The Pattern Library
KNITTING

Editor
Amy Carroll

Contributor
Dorothea Hall

BALLANTINE BOOKS · NEW YORK

First published in Great Britain in 1981 by
Ebury Press, National Magazine House,
72 Broadwick Street, London W1V 2BP

The Pattern Library KNITTING was conceived, edited
and designed by Dorling Kindersley Limited,
9 Henrietta Street, London WC2

Library of Congress Catalog Card Number: 81–66168

ISBN 0–345–29595–1

Manufactured in the United States of America

First Ballantine Books Edition: October 1981
10 9 8 7 6 5 4 3 2 1

Contents

❖

❖

Introduction

The joy and satisfaction in hand knitting combined with economy makes it one of the most popular crafts today. In the past, yarn was home-spun – shearing, carding and spinning took months of preparation and knitting patterns were very seldom written down, but were passed on by word of mouth.

The introduction of man-made yarns created a tremendous interest in all hand knitting and, today, we have an immense range of very practical yarns to choose from, in beautiful colors and textures. Many stitch patterns were created simultaneously in different parts of the world, while others, such as Arabian two-color knitting, are indigenous to certain places. However, most of the single-colored stitch patterns we use today developed largely from the distinctive patterns woven into the knitted Guernseys of the fishermen of Great Britain; from Sherringham and Whitby, to Aberdeen, Inishmore and Portmadoc. These densely knit regional patterns contrast strongly with the cobwebby effect of a Shetland shawl, Fair Isle patterns knitted in browns and fawns of natural-colored fleece and the deep embossed cables and bobbles of Aran knitting.

The stitch patterns in this volume range from the traditional rib, ripple, cable and trellis to basketweave and bobble, and include up-to-date techniques for knitting many other patterns from pictorial colorwork to Swiss darning, appliqué and honeycombing.

The aim throughout the book is to give hand knitters the confidence to adapt and transform existing patterns with success. You will need little more than needles and yarns to create fashion garments for you and your family, or colorful decorations for your home.

BASIC TECHNIQUES

NEEDLES

Knitting needles are machine-made from plastic-coated lightweight aluminum, steel, plastic or wood. You can buy pairs of needles with knobs at one end for knitting back and forth in rows; double-pointed needles, in sets of three or more, and circular needles for knitting "in the round"; short cable needles for holding stitches in twisted cable patterns. All needles are graded in different sizes according to their diameter, from 2mm to 25mm. Buy good quality needles with well-shaped points.

YARNS

In addition to wool and the many synthetic yarns now produced, you can knit with cotton, string, ribbon, rafia or any pliable fiber.

Fibers used to produce hand-knitting yarns generally fall into two main categories – natural and man-made – while many commercial yarns are classified according to their construction, eg. 3-4-ply and crêpe.

Ply Fibers are first spun into single threads, called a ply, and then the threads are twisted together to make a specific yarn. Note that "ply" does not indicate a standard thickness of thread, but refers directly to the number of single threads used in making a specific yarn.

Which yarn? It is essential to choose the most appropriate yarn and stitch pattern to suit your specific needs. Generally, firm, windproof fabrics are produced with thick yarn and relatively small needles; soft, yet thick and warm fabrics require lightly twisted middle-weight yarn and bigger needles, while baby wear demands soft, washable yarn and small needles.

Yarn swatches

2-3 ply wool

baby wool quick knit

4-ply botany

Shetland

knitting worsted

thick knitting worsted

chunky

synthetic crêpe

wool crêpe

double crêpe

mohair

angora

novelty tweed

bouclé

poodle

knitting cottons

chenille

cotton slub

lurex

metallic mix

7

CASTING ON

All hand knitting starts with a number of loops being cast on to one needle and further rows are then worked into these loops.

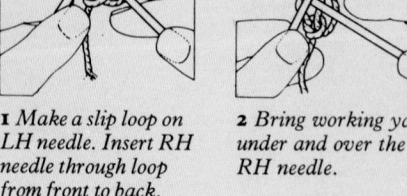

1 *Make a slip loop on LH needle. Insert RH needle through loop from front to back.*

2 *Bring working yarn under and over the RH needle.*

3 *Draw loop through slip stitch and transfer to LH needle. Repeat steps 1 and 2.*

BASIC KNIT STITCH

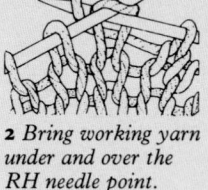

1 *With yarn at back, insert RH needle from front to back into first stitch on LH needle.*

2 *Bring working yarn under and over the RH needle point.*

3 *Draw loop through, discarding worked stitch on LH needle. Continue in this way to end of row.*

Complete the first row and turn the work around. Take the needle carrying the stitches into the left hand and the empty needle in the right. With back of work now facing, begin a new row.

BASIC PURL STITCH

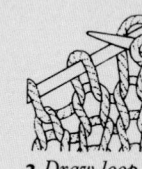

1 *With yarn at front, insert RH needle from back to front into first stitch on LH needle.*

2 *Bring working yarn over and around RH needle point.*

3 *Draw loop through, discarding worked stitch on LH needle. Continue in this way to end of row.*

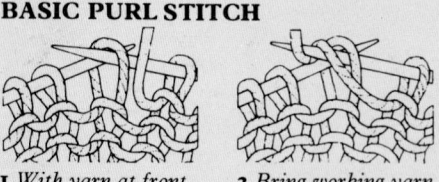

Changing from a knit stitch
to a purl stitch (eg. "ribbing"); k3, bring yarn to front of work, p3.

Changing from a purl stitch
to a knit stitch (eg. "ribbing"); p3, take yarn to back of work, k3.

8

CASTING OFF

Secure the stitches of your finished piece of knitting by casting off. This is usually done on a knit row but the same method is used when purling. For casting off in rib, remember to position your yarn correctly before knitting or purling the two working stitches.

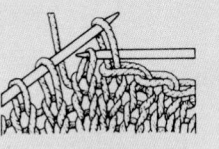 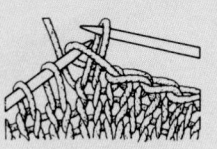 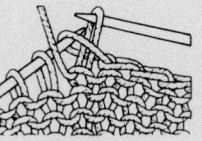

To cast off k-wise
1 *Knit first 2 stitches and insert point of LH needle into first st.*

2 *Lift first stitch over second and off needle. K 1 stitch and continue to lift one stitch over another to end of row.*

To cast off p-wise
Purl first 2 stitches and continue as for knit row.

SELVEDGES AND SEAMS

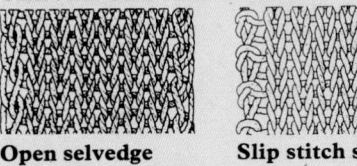 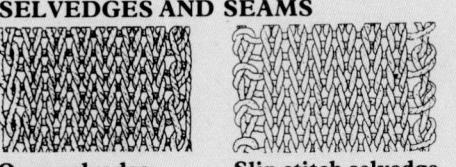 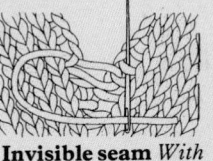

Open selvedge
(use on unseamed edges)
Slip first and last sts on every k row knitwise. Purl all sts in p row.

Slip stitch selvedge
(use on seamed edges)
Slip first st purlwise and knit last st on every row.

Invisible seam *With RS facing, pick up 1 st and pull yarn through. Pick up next st from opposite side; repeat.*

INCREASING

"Invisible" increasing doesn't leave a hole in the knitted fabric and is generally used in the construction of garments. Use (**inc 1**) method mainly for shaping side edges and (**M1, k up 1,** or **p up 1**) for tailored shaping made within the body of the knitting.

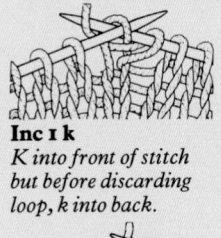 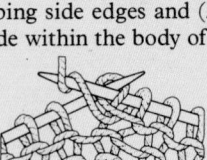 

Inc 1 k
K into front of stitch but before discarding loop, k into back.

Inc 1 p
P into front of stitch but before discarding loop, p into back.

Completed increase
2 stitches from 1; purlwise on left, knitwise on right.

 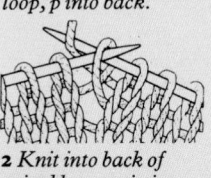 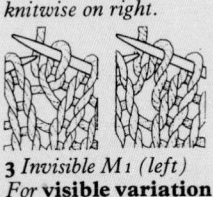

M1 k-wise
1 *Insert LH needle under running thread between 2 stitches.*

2 *Knit into back of raised loop, twisting it so as not to leave a hole in the fabric.*

3 *Invisible M1 (left)*
For **visible variation** *(right) knit into front of running thread.*

9

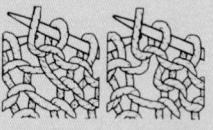

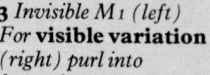

M1 p-wise
1 *Insert LH needle under running thread between 2 stitches.*

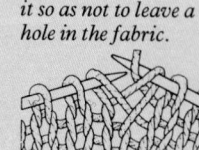

2 *Purl into back of raised loop, twisting it so as not to leave a hole in the fabric.*

3 *Invisible M1 (left)* **For visible variation** *(right) purl into front of running thread.*

Knit up one (k up 1) is often referred to as a "lifted increase" since it picks up the loop of stitch below next to be worked; it is barely visible in the finished fabric.

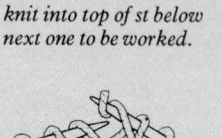

1 *With RH needle knit into top of st below next one to be worked.*

2 *Knit next stitch on LH needle; continue to end of row.*

Purl up one (p up 1) is a "lifted increase" made by purling into top loop of stitch in row below. As in k up 1, the new stitch is made on the RH needle.

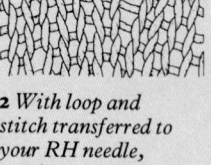

1 *With RH needle purl into top of st below next one to be worked.*

2 *Purl next stitch on LH needle; continue to end of row.*

DECORATIVE INCREASING

This method of increasing forms eyelet holes in the fabric and may be used not only for practical purposes, such as buttonholes, or to highlight a raglan seam, but mainly as the basis for all lace knitting. Work lace patterns by increasing stitches, using either (**yfwd/yo**) or (**yrn**) method, and decreasing in the same row in order to compensate for the made stitches.

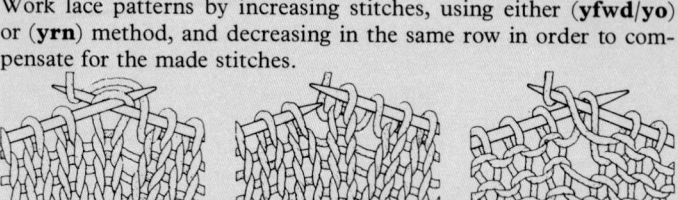

Yfwd/yo
1 *Bring yarn forward, loop it over RH needle and knit next stitch.*

2 *With loop and stitch transferred to your RH needle, continue to end of row.*

3 *On following row, purl into loop in the usual way. Work in pattern to end of row.*

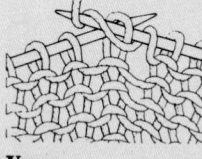

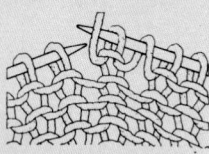

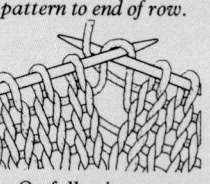

Yrn
1 *Take yarn round RH needle to front of work. Purl next stitch.*

2 *With loop and stitch transferred to your RH needle, continue to end of row.*

3 *On following row, knit into loop in the usual way. Work in pattern to end of row.*

DECREASING

The simplest way to decrease is to knit or purl 2 stitches together (**k2 tog/p2 tog**) at either end of the row or at any given point. To make a special feature of decreasing, use the slip stitch method where the decreases are worked in pairs, one slanting to the left and the other to the right, as on a raglan sleeve.

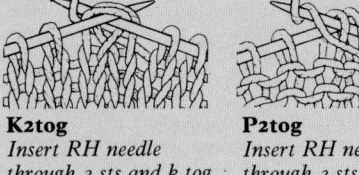 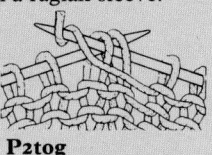 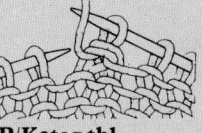

K2tog
Insert RH needle through 2 sts and k tog as 1 st. Dec slants L to R.

P2tog
Insert RH needle through 2 sts and p tog as 1 st. Dec slants L to R.

P/K2tog tbl
Purl or knit 2 stitches together through back of loop, for decrease to slant R to L.

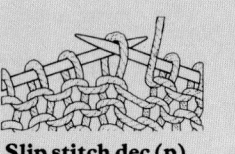 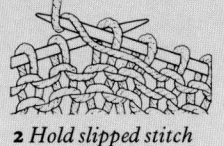 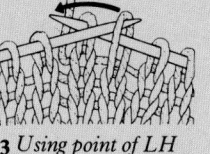

Slip stitch dec (k) (sl 1, k1, psso)
1 *Slip next st from LH needle onto RH needle.*

2 *Hold slipped stitch and knit next stitch in usual way.*

3 *Using point of LH needle, lift slipped stitch over knit stitch and off RH needle. Dec slants R to L.*

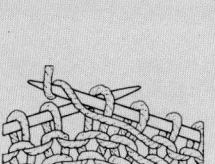

Slip stitch dec (p) (sl 1, p1, psso)
1 *Slip next stitch from LH needle onto RH needle.*

2 *Hold slipped stitch and purl next stitch in usual way.*

3 *Using point of LH needle, lift slipped stitch over purl stitch and off RH needle. Dec slants L to R on RS.*

MAKING A CHAIN EYELET (k2, yo, k2tog)

Prevent uneven selvedges by starting eyelet patterns 2 sts in from beginning of row and finishing 2 sts from end. To keep number of sts in repeat constant, increases and decreases should be equal.

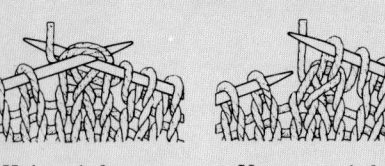 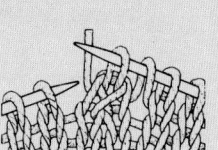 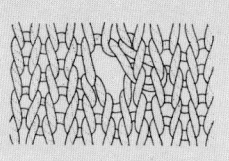

1 *Knit 2 stitches, yarn over, knit 2 together.*

2 *Yarn over stitch replaces knit 2 together.*

3 *Detail of finished chain eyelet.*

USING A CABLE NEEDLE (cn)

For twisting 2 or more stitches, a double-pointed cable needle should be used. The stitches to be twisted are slipped onto it and held, either at the front or back of the work, until ready to be knitted. Stitches held at the front will twist cable from right to left while those held at the back will twist cable from left to right.

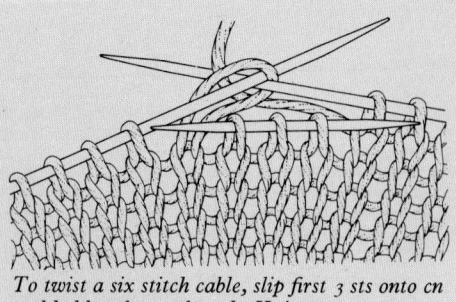

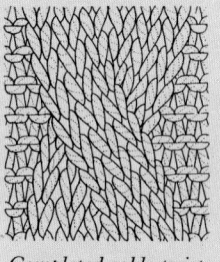

To twist a six stitch cable, slip first 3 sts onto cn and hold at front of work. Knit next 3 sts, then knit first 3 sts off cn.

Completed cable twist from right to left.

ADDING NEW COLORS

Add a new ball of yarn or another color, as in horizontal stripes at the beginning of a row; the yarn is either broken off or carried up the side of the work until it is needed. For more intricate colorwork, eg. "jacquard", new yarn may be introduced at the beginning or in the middle of a row. Darn all loose ends neatly into the selvedge or through back of work.

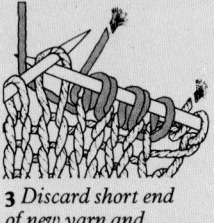

Beginning new row
1 *Insert RH needle into 1st stitch on LH needle. K 1 st using old and new yarns tog.*

2 *Leave old yarn at the back and knit next 2 stitches with 2 strands of new yarn.*

3 *Discard short end of new yarn and continue to knit. Pick up old yarn from side edge if required later.*

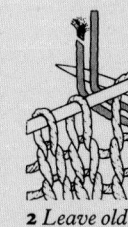

Middle of row
1 *Insert RH needle into next st on LH needle. Wrap new yarn over RH needle, k st.*

2 *Leave old yarn at the back and knit next 2 stitches with 2 strands of new yarn.*

3 *Discard short end of new yarn and continue to knit. Use new and old yarns as required in pattern.*

STRANDING YARN

Use the stranding method for working narrow stripes, small dot or check repeats, and for traditional Fair Isle patterns with 2 colors in a row. Strand yarn over 2 to 5 stitches but weave in over 5, keeping an even tension throughout.

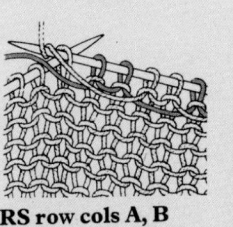

RS row cols A, B
With A, k 2, leave at back. Carry B loosely across back, k 2.
On a p row, *carry yarn across front.*

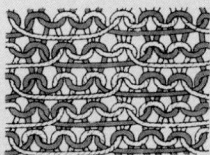
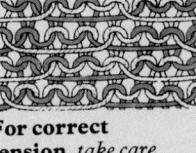

For correct tension, *take care not to pull loose stranding yarn too tight on WS.*

WEAVING YARN

Use weaving technique for carrying colored yarns over more than 5 sts. This will avoid making long, unsightly strands of yarn which can catch and distort the fabric. Remember, stranding and weaving will produce double thickness.

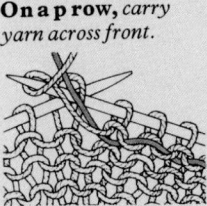

RS row cols A, B
1 *With both yarns at back, B in LH and A in RH, k 1. On 2nd and alt sts insert needle and bring B in LH over A.*

2 *With A, complete k st keeping B below A.*
On a p row *weave yarns in same way carrying them at front of work.*

COLORSLIP

These intricate-looking patterns have a simple working method based on combining 2-color horizontal stripes with slip stitches. Only 1 color at a time is knitted. Carry any yarns not in use up side of work.

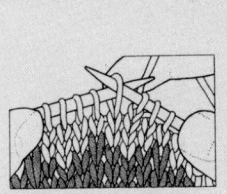

RS row: *With 2nd color yarn at back, slip next stitch p-wise off LH needle.*

WS row: *Carrying 2nd color yarn loosely across front, p next st in usual way.*

CROSSING YARN

Work large blocks of color, eg. diagonal or wide vertical stripes or jacquard motifs, with separate bobbins of yarn for each color repeated in a row, twisting them on WS as color change is made.

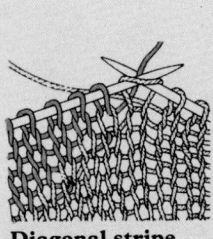

Diagonal stripe L to R: *Cross 1st col in front of 2nd; pick up 2nd, k.*
P row: *colors encroach.*

Diagonal stripe R to L: *Cross 1st color behind 2nd; pick up 2nd and p.*
K row: *colors encroach.*

PUTTING THE STITCH PATTERNS TO USE

Before you begin to knit any item you should always work a tension sample first. This is necessary whether you intend to use a printed pattern; substitute the given stitch and/or yarn, with another; or, use your own design.

TENSION

Tension involves the relationship between yarn and needles and the way your fingers control the yarn. With practice you will notice, for example, that thicker yarns require a slacker control of tension while thinner yarns require a tighter control. Any tension variation within a garment will give an uneven appearance. By calculating stitches and rows, your tension sample will also show whether the yarn and needles you are using will make up into the size, shape and weight you require. Printed patterns give a tension guide stating the number of stitches and rows to a 4in. square using the recommended yarn and needles.

To make a tension sample, begin by working a square slightly larger than 4in. Place it on a flat surface and, using pins, mark out the tension measurement given in the pattern.

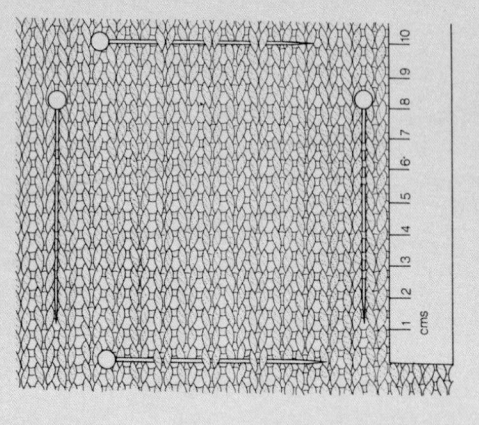

Count the rows and stitches between the pins and if they are the same as in the pattern, then your tension is correct. If there are too many stitches between pins, then your tension is too tight and you should try one, or more size larger needles. Too few stitches, and you should try one, or more, size smaller.

SUBSTITUTING ONE STITCH FOR ANOTHER

This opens up many new design opportunities providing that the stitch you substitute is of a similar type to the original one given in the pattern, and that the "multiple of stitches" will fit. Patterns combining different stitches within a row require a specific number or multiple of stitches so that the pattern repeats evenly across a row. For instance, a particular pattern may call for a multiple of 8 stitches plus 2. You should then cast on 8, 16, 24, 32 sts or more according to your required width, plus 2 sts, which go at either end of the row, to be used for the seams. Using the recommended yarn, work a tension sample in the new stitch, and at the same time, calculate the multiple of stitches and adjust if necessary. With small multiples it may be possible to equally divide any left-over stitches to the side edges. You may also substitute one yarn for another, providing you follow the same principle of choosing one from the same category as the original, eg. 4-ply or mohair, and working a tension sample first.

DESIGNING WITH A TENSION GRID

For your first attempt at designing a knitted garment, one of the best methods is to use the tension grid technique to establish how many stitches are required for pattern and shape (see pp9, 11 for increasing and decreasing). Begin with a simple stitch pattern and with yarn and needles of your choice, work a tension sample, counting the exact number of rows and stitches.

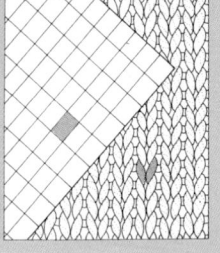 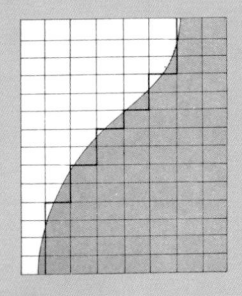

To get an accurate outline of the shape, draw on a large sheet of tracing paper a grid to match the size of your tension stitch. Note that the knitted stitch is usually rectangular. Place paper pattern under grid, trace off outline, stepping curves to match grid lines.

You will now see from your grid exactly how many stitches you will need to cast on and precisely where to make increases and decreases for shaping. Economize by using the same grid for further pattern components by over-tracing in contrasting colors.

ESTIMATING YARN QUANTITIES

If you intend using a spinner's yarn, a reliable method of estimating quantity is to take a printed pattern of the same style and use the suggested quantities as a guide. Another method is to knit a ball of yarn in your chosen stitch, measure the area, then estimate the total area of your design and calculate how much it will take to complete it.

NEEDLE AND YARN TABLE

2mm	2-ply, 3-ply, baby yarn	**5**	thick knitting worsted.
2¼		**5½**	
2¾		**6**	
2¾	4-ply, baby quick-knits	**6½**	chunky yarn, mohair
3		**7**	
3¼		**7½**	
3¼	knitting worsted	**8**	heavyweight yarns
3¾		**9**	
4		**10**	
4½			

ABBREVIATIONS

alt	alternately	**patt**	pattern
BC	back cross	**psso**	pass slipped stitch over
beg	beginning	**p2sso**	pass 2 slipped stitches over
BKC	back knit cross	**p up**	pick up and purl
col	color	**p-wise**	purlwise
cont	continu(e/ing)	**R**	right
cn	cable needle	**rem**	remain(ing)
dec	decreas(e/ing)	**rep**	repeat
dpn	double-pointed needle	**RH**	right-hand
DL	drop loop	**RN**	right needle
FC	front cross	**RS**	right side
FKC	front knit cross	**RT**	right twist
foll	following	**SBC**	single back cross
g st	garter stitch	**SFC**	single front cross
inc	increas(e/ing)	**sl**	slip
k	knit	**sl st**	slip stitch
k up	pick up and knit	**st(s)**	stitches
k1-b	knit one into back	**st st**	stockinette stitch
k-wise	knitwise	**tbl**	through back of loop(s)
L	left	**tog**	together
LH	left-hand	**WS**	wrong side
LN	left needle	**wyib**	with yarn in back
LT	left twist	**wyif**	with yarn in front
M1	make one	**ybk**	yarn back
MB	make bobble	**yfwd/yo**	yarn forward/yarn over
m-st	moss stitch	**yon**	yarn over needle
no(s)	number(s)	**yrn**	yarn round needle
p	purl	**y2rn**	yarn twice round needle

Symbols

A star * shown in a pattern row denotes that the stitches shown after this sign must be repeated from that point.

Round brackets ( ), enclosing a particular stitch combination, denote that the stitch combination must be repeated in the order shown.

KNIT & PURL

These two simple stitches form the basis of all knitting stitch patterns (see p8). The innumerable patterns you can make by using either one or a combination of both stitches may be smoothly or richly textured. The pattern repeat may also vary in size from one or two nubbly stitches through ribs and ripples to wide chevron stripes or lattice bars.

Double basket

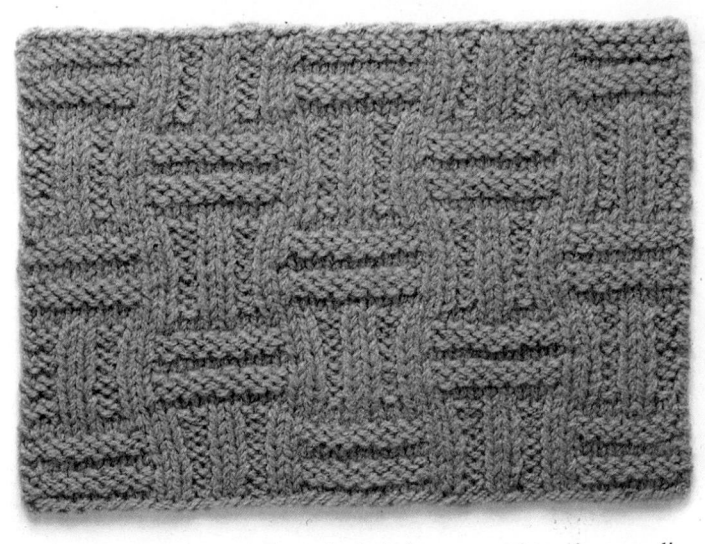

Materials Chunky, novelty mix, knitting worsted wool or acrylic for warm, rugged textured outdoor wear.

Uses All-over design for hooded poncho, man's zipped jacket, junior blouson, blanket or rug square.

Multiple of 18 sts plus 10.

Row 1 (RS) *K11, p2, k2, p2, k1; rep from *, end k10.

Row 2 P1, k8, p1, *p1, (k2, p2) twice, k8, p1; rep from *.

Row 3 *K1, p8, (k2, p2) twice, k1; rep from *, end k1, p8, k1.

Row 4 P10, *p1, k2, p2, k2, p11; rep from *.

Rows 5, 6, 7 and 8 Repeat rows 1, 2, 3 and 4.

Row 9 Knit.

Row 10 (P2, k2) twice, p2, *p10, (k2, p2) twice; rep from *.

Row 11 *(K2, p2) twice, k2, p8; rep from *, end (k2, p2) twice, k2.

Row 12 (P2, k2) twice, p2, *k8 (p2, k2) twice, p2; rep from *.

Row 13 *(K2, p2) twice, k10; rep from *, end (k2, p2) twice, k2.

Rows 14, 15, 16 and 17 Repeat rows 10, 11, 12 and 13.

Row 18 Purl.

Repeat rows 1 to 18.

Reversible diagonal

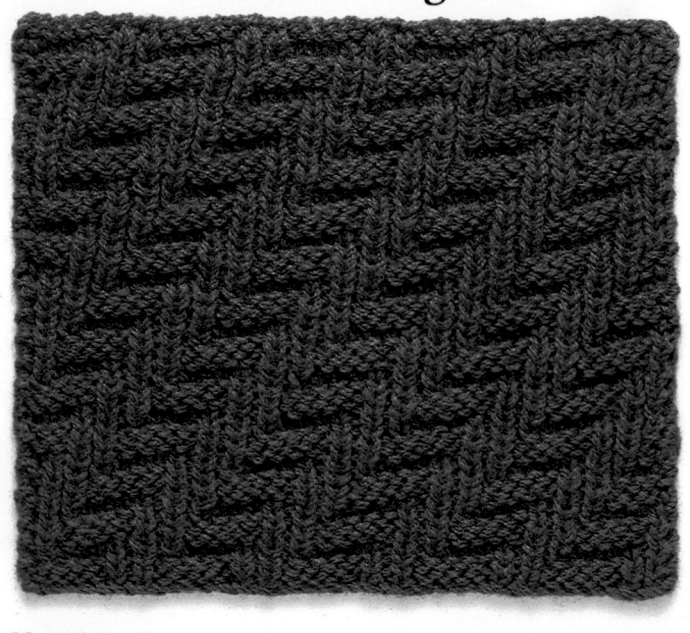

Materials Chunky or double crêpe for stitch clarity; tweedy wool for country wear.

Uses All-over design for jacket, poncho or chequered traveling rug; inset cape panel or all-over pattern for sporty knee socks.

Multiple of 8 sts.

Row 1 *K1, p1, k1, p5; rep from *.

Row 2 *and all other even-numbered rows.* Knit all k sts and purl all p sts.

Row 3 K1, p1, *k5, p1, k1, p1; rep from *, end k5, p1.

Row 5 K1, *p5, k1, p1, k1; rep from *, end p5, k1, p1.

Row 7 *K5, p1, k1, p1; rep from *.

Row 9 P4, *k1, p1, k1, p5; rep from *, end (k1, p1) twice.

Row 11 K3, *p1, k1, p1, k5; rep from *, end p1, k1, p1, k2.

Row 13 P2, *k1, p1, k1, p5; rep from *, end k1, p1, k1, p3.

Row 15 K1, *p1, k1, p1, k5; rep from *, end p1, k1, p1, k4.

Row 16 See row 2.

Repeat rows 1 to 16.

Sailor's rib

Materials Chunky or Aran-type wool for warmth; novelty or random-dyed yarn for a sporty effect.

Uses Coat or sweater inset panel; all-over repeat for cardigan, waistcoat, toddler's togs or child's knee socks.

Multiple of 5 sts plus 1.

Row 1 (RS) k1-b, *p1, k2, p1, k1-b; rep from *.
Row 2 P1, *k1, p2, k1, p1; rep from *.
Row 3 K1-b, *p4, k1-b; rep from *.
Row 4 P1, *k4, p1; rep from *.
Repeat rows 1 to 4.

Seeded rib check

Materials Medium-weight yarn for a dense-textured fabric and warm casual wear.

Uses Jersey or pullover inset panel; all-over design for toddler's togs or blanket square.

Multiple of 4 sts plus 3.

Row 1 K3, *p1, k3; rep from *.
Row 2 K1, *p1, k3; rep from *, end p1, k1.
Rows 3 and 5 Repeat row 1.
Rows 4 and 6 Repeat row 2.
Rows 7, 9 and 11 Repeat row 2.
Rows 8, 10 and 12 Repeat row 1.
Repeat rows 1 to 12.

Double pennant

Materials Aran-type or knitting worsted wool for an outdoor look; smooth light-weight wool, cotton or lurex for evening.
Uses Jersey yoke, inset sleeve or body panel; band, stripe or all-over pattern for suit, dress or skirt.

Multiple of 10 sts plus 1.

Row 1 (RS) K1, *p7, k3; rep from *.
Row 2 *P4, k6; rep from *, end p1.
Row 3 K1, *p5, k5; rep from *.
Row 4 *P6, k4; rep from *, end p1.
Row 5 K1, *p3, k7; rep from *.
Row 6 *P8, k2; rep from *, end p1.
Row 7 K1, *p1, k9; rep from *.
Rows 8, 9, 10, 11, 12 and 13 Repeat rows 6, 5, 4, 3, 2, 1.
Row 14 P2, *k7, p3; rep from *, end k7, p2.

Row 15 *K3, p7; rep from *, end k1.
Row 16 P1, *k6, p4; rep from *.
Row 17 *K5, p5; rep from *, end k1.
Row 18 P1, *k4, p6; rep from *.
Row 19 *K7, p3; rep from *, end k1.
Row 20 P1, *k2, p8; rep from *.
Row 21 *K9, p1; rep from *, end k1.
Rows 22, 23, 24, 25, 26, 27 and 28 Repeat rows 20, 19, 18, 17, 16, 15 and 14.
Repeat rows 1 to 28.

Chevron

Materials 4-ply, novelty mix or tweedy wool for a sporty look; bouclé or angora for warmth.

Uses Inset dress or sweater panel or all-over design for a classic-style slipover; baby's sleeping bag or carriage cover.

Multiple of 8 sts.

Row 1 *K1, p7; rep from *.
Row 2 *and all even-numbered rows.* Knit all k sts and purl all p sts.
Row 3 K2, *p5, k3; rep from *, end p5, k1.
Row 5 K3, *p3, k5; rep from *, end p3, k2.
Row 7 K4, *p1, k7; rep from *, end p1, k3.

Row 9 *P1, k7; rep from *.
Row 11 P2, *k5, p3; rep from *, end k5, p1.
Row 13 P3, *k3, p5; rep from *, end k3, p2.
Row 15 P4, *k1, p7; rep from *, end k1, p3.
Row 16 See row 2.
Repeat rows 1 to 16.

Steep diagonal rib

Materials Knitting worsted or tweedy wool for a sporty, deep-textured fabric.

Uses All-over design for father and son pullover, tie or zipped blouson jacket.

Multiple of 6 sts.

Row 1 *P3, k3; rep from *.

Row 2 *and all other even-numbered rows.* Knit all knit sts and purl all purl sts.

Row 3 P2, *k3, p3; rep from *, end k3, p1.

Row 5 P1, *k3, p3; rep from *, end k3, p2.

Row 7 *K3, p3; rep from *.

Row 9 K2, *p3, k3; rep from *, end p3, k1.

Row 11 K1, *p3, k3; rep from *, end p3, k2.

Row 12 See row 2.

Repeat rows 1 to 12.

Basket rib

Materials Chunky knitting or double crêpe wool for a rich nubbly texture and warmth; synthetic yarn for washability.

Uses Sweater or slipover inset panel; all-over repeat for baby's coat or sleeping bag.

Multiple of 4 sts plus 1.

Row 1 (RS) K1, *p1, k1; rep from *.

Row 2 K2, *p1, k3; rep from *, end p1, k2.

Row 3 P2, *k1, p1; rep from *, end k1, p2.

Row 4 P1, *k1, p1; rep from *.

Row 5 K1, *p3, k1; rep from *.

Row 6 P1, *k3, p1; rep from *.

Repeat rows 1 to 6.

Dotted chevron

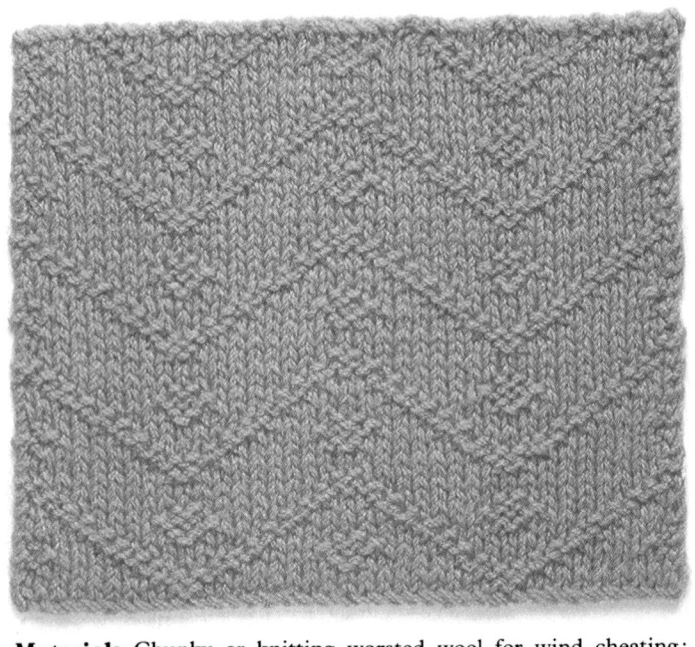

Materials Chunky or knitting worsted wool for wind cheating; tweedy wool for cruiser furnishing.

Uses Inset sweater or coat panel; Aran-style cushion cover or bunk-bed set.

Multiple of 18 sts.

Row 1 (RS) *K8, p2, k8; rep from *.
Row 2 *P7, k4, p7; rep from *.
Row 3 *P1, k5, p2, k2, p2, k5, p1; rep from *.
Row 4 *K2, p3, k2, p4, k2, p3, k2; rep from *.
Row 5 *P1, k3, p2, k6, p2, k3, p1; rep from *.
Row 6 *P3, (k2, p3) 3 times; rep from *.
Row 7 *K2, p2, k3, p4, k3, p2, k2; rep from *.
Row 8 *P1, k2, (p5, k2) twice, p1; rep from *.
Row 9 *P2, k14, p2; rep from *.
Row 10 *K1, p16, k1; rep from *.
Repeat rows 1 to 10.

Vandyke check

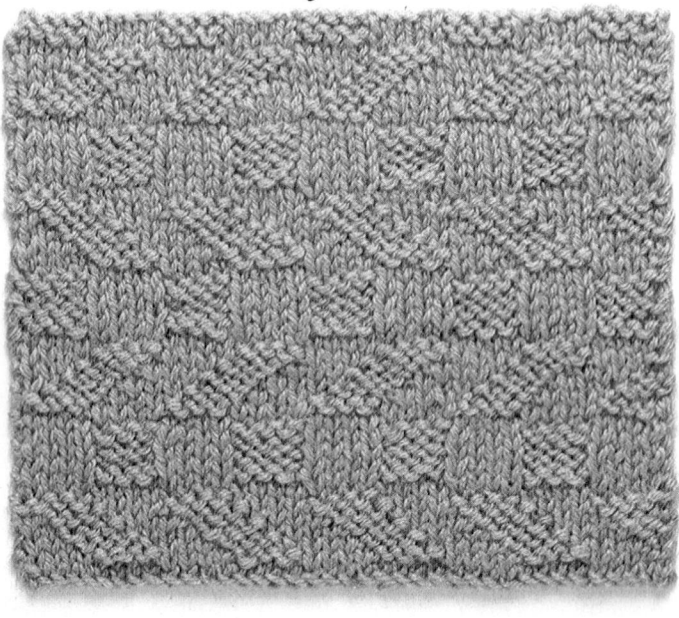

Materials Crêpe or knitting worsted wool to show off stitch pattern; tweedy wool or angora for wintry days.

Uses Overall pattern for blanket, cushion or shoulder bag; inset coat or sweater panel.

Multiple of 8 sts.

Row 1 (RS) Knit.
Row 2 *K4, p4; rep from *.
Row 3 P1, *k4, p4; rep from *, end last rep p3 instead of p4.
Row 4 K2, *p4, k4; rep from *, end last rep k2, instead of k4.
Row 5 P3, *k4, p4; rep from *, end last rep p1 instead of p4.
Row 6 *P4, k4; rep from *.
Row 7 Knit.
Rows 8, 9, 10 and 11 *K4, p4, rep from *.
Row 12 Purl.

Row 13 *P4, k4; rep from *.
Row 14 K1, *p4, k4; rep from *, end last rep k3 instead of k4.
Row 15 P2, *k4, p4; rep from *, end last rep p2 instead of p4.
Row 16 K3, *p4, k4; rep from *, end last rep k1 instead of k4.
Row 17 *K4, p4; rep from *.
Row 18 Purl.
Rows 19, 20, 21 and 22 *P4, k4; rep from *.
Repeat rows 1 to 22.

Diamond check

Materials 4-ply wool, novelty mix or acrylic for town wear.
Uses All-over pattern for cardigan, waistcoat, socks, baby's hooded cape or bed cover.

Multiple of 18 sts plus 2.

Row 1 (RS) P2, *k4, p4, k2, p2, k4, p2; rep from *.
Row 2 K3, *p4, k2, p2, k2, p4, k4; rep from *, end last repeat k3.
Row 3 K2, *p2, k4, p4, k4, p2, k2; rep from *.
Row 4 P1, *k4, (p4, k2) twice, p2; rep from *, end k1.
Row 5 P2, *k2, p2, k8, p2, k2, p2; rep from *.
Row 6 K1, *p2, k4, p6, k2, p2, k2; rep from *, end p1.
Row 7 K2, *p2, k2, p2, k4, (p2, k2) twice; rep from *.
Row 8 P1, *k2, p2, k2, p6, k4, p2; rep from *, end k1.

Rows 9, 11 and 12 Repeat rows 5, 3 and 2.
Row 10 K1, *p2, (k2, p4) twice, k4; rep from *, end p1.
Row 13 P2, *k4, p2, k2, p4, k4, p2; rep from *.
Row 14 P5, *(k2, p2) twice, k2, p8; rep from *, end last repeat p5.
Row 15 K4, *(p2, k2) twice, p4, k6; rep from *, end last repeat k4.
Row 16 P3, *(k2, p2) 3 times, k2, p4; rep from *, end last repeat p3.
Row 17 K4, *p4, (k2, p2) twice, k6; rep from *, end last repeat k4.
Row 18 Repeat row 14.
Repeat rows 1 to 18.

Basketweave

Materials Knitting worsted or random-dyed yarn for a sporty look; synthetic or cotton for wash and wear.

Uses All-over pattern for bomber-style jacket, tabard or baby's bed cover; cushion cover, placemat or bathroom set.

Multiple of 8 sts plus 5.
Row 1 (RS) Knit.
Row 2 K5, *p3, k5; rep from *.
Row 3 P5, *k3, p5; rep from *.
Row 4 Repeat row 2.
Row 5 Knit.
Row 6 K1, *p3, k5; rep from *, end last rep k1 instead of k5.
Row 7 P1, *k3, p5; rep from *, end last rep p1 instead of p5.
Row 8 Repeat row 6.
Repeat rows 1 to 8.

Long rib check

Materials Knitting worsted wool, crêpe or acrylic yarn for everyday wear.

Uses All-over pattern for mother or father cardigan, baby togs or school wear.

Multiple of 4 sts plus 2.
Rows 1, 3 and 5 K2, *p2, k2; rep from *.
Rows 2, 4 and 6 P2, *k2, p2; rep from *.
Rows 7, 9 and 11 P2, *k2, p2; rep from *.
Rows 8, 10 and 12 K2, *p2, k2; rep from *.
Repeat rows 1 to 12.

Lozenge brocade

Materials Medium-weight yarn for light-textured casual wear; chunky yarn for furnishing.

Uses Inset panel or band for mother and daughter sweater or all-over design for sleeveless overblouse; cushion set or rug.

Multiple of 12 sts plus 1.

Row 1 (RS) K1, *p1, k9, p1, k1; rep from *.

Row 2 K1, *p1, k1, p7, k1, p1, k1; rep from *.

Row 3 K1, *p1, k1, p1, k5, (p1, k1) twice; rep from *.

Row 4 P1, *(p1, k1) twice, p3, k1, p1, k1, p2; rep from *.

Row 5 K1, *k2, (p1, k1) 3 times, p1, k3; rep from *.

Row 6 P1, *p3, (k1, p1) twice, k1, p4; rep from *.

Row 7 K1, *k4, p1, k1, p1, k5; rep from *.

Row 8 Repeat row 6.

Row 9 Repeat row 5.

Row 10 Repeat row 4.

Row 11 Repeat row 3.

Row 12 Repeat row 2.

Repeat rows 1 to 12.

Zigzag stitch

Materials Smooth medium-weight yarn for a classic style.
Uses All-over pattern or inset panel for boy or girl sweater, jacket or dress.

Multiple of 6 sts.
Row 1 (WS) *and all other WS rows* Purl.
Row 2 *K3, p3; rep from *.
Row 4 P1, *k3, p3; rep from *, end last rep p2 instead of p3.
Row 6 P2, *k3, p3; rep from *, end last rep p1 instead of p3.
Row 8 *P3, k3; rep from *.
Row 10 P2, *k3, p3; rep from *, end last rep p1 instead of p3.
Row 12 P1, *k3, p3; rep from *, end last rep p2 instead of p3.
Repeat rows 1 to 12.

Double moss stitch

Materials 3- or 4-ply wool or synthetic mixes for school wear.
Uses All-over pattern for child's button-through cardigan, pullover or snug-fitting hat with matching scarf and gloves.

Multiple of 4 sts.
Rows 1 and 2 *K2, p2; rep from *.
Rows 3 and 4 *P2, k2; rep from *.
Repeat rows 1 to 4.

CABLE

*All cable stitch patterns are made by
moving stitches from one position in a row to
another. For lightly embossed, lattice or ribbed patterns,
two stitches may be twisted simply on the needle. For deeply
embossed, rope or plaited patterns you will find it easier to
twist three or more stitches with a cable needle (see p12).
Patterns range from a single twisted rope through linked
chains and leaf rib to broad interlaced bands.*

Four rib cable

Materials Oiled or Aran-type yarn for sailing; tweed, mohair or poodle wool for holiday wear.
Uses Sweater inset panel, or mix with other pattern panels for loose-fitting guernsey; belted knee length jacket or mitts.

Panel of 17 sts.
Note *Back Cross (BC) : sl 1 st to cn and hold at back, k2, then p1 from cn. Front Cross (FC) : sl 2 sts to cn and hold at front, p1, then k2 from cn.*
Row 1 (WS) (K2, p2) twice, k1, (p2, k2) twice.
Row 2 P2, k2, p2, sl next 3 sts to cn and hold at *back*, k2, sl purl st from cn back to LH needle and purl it, then k2 from cn; p2, k2, p2.
Row 3 Repeat row 1.
Row 4 P2, FC, BC, p1, FC, BC, p2.
Row 5 (K3, p4) twice, k3.
Row 6 P3, sl next 2 sts to cn and hold at back, k2, then k2 from cn; p3, sl next 2 sts to cn and hold at front, k2, then k2 from cn; p3.
Row 7 Repeat row 5.
Row 8 P2, BC, FC, p1, BC, FC, p2.
Row 9 Repeat row 1.
Row 10 P2, k2, p2, sl the next 3 sts to cn and hold at *front*, k2, then sl the purl st from cn back to LH needle and purl it, then k2 from cn; p2, k2, p2.
Rows 11 to 16 Repeat rows 3 to 8. Repeat rows 1 to 16.

Five rib cable

Materials Aran or knitting worsted wool for extra warmth; dishcloth cotton for fun furnishing.

Uses All-over pattern for seaman's polo neck sweater, jersey yoke or inset panel for gloves and socks; bed cover or bolster.

Center panel of 14 sts.

Note *Front Cross (FC) : sl 2 sts to cn and hold at front, k2, then k2 from cn.*
Back Cross (BC) : sl 2 sts to cn and hold at back, k2, then k2 from cn.

Rows 1 and 3 (WS) K2, p10, k2.
Row 2 P2, k2, (FC) twice, p2.
Row 4 P2 (BC) twice, k2, p2.
Repeat rows 1 to 4.

Eight stitch cable

Materials Novelty mix, oiled or knitting worsted wool for sea winds.

Uses Inset panel for fisherman's jersey or girl's hooded poncho with matching scarf and hat.

Center panel of 12 sts.

Rows 1 and 3 (WS) K2, p8, k2.
Row 2 P2, k8, p2.
Row 4 P2, sl next 4 sts to cn and hold at back (or at front); k4, then k4 from cn, p2.
Rows 5, 7 and 9 As rows 1 and 3.
Rows 6, 8 and 10 As row 2.
Repeat rows 1 to 10.

Eccentric cable

Materials Mohair, poodle or chunky yarn for autumn wear.
Uses Inset front panel for classic-style button-through cardigan, repeat pattern for sweater dress or full-length cape.

Center panel of 10 sts.
Rows 1 and 3 (WS) K2, p6, k2.
Row 2 P2, k6, p2.
Row 4 P2, sl next 3 sts to cn and hold at back (or at front); k3, then k3 from cn, p2.
Rows 5, 7, 9, 11, 13, 15 and 17 As rows 1 and 3.
Rows 6 and 8 As row 2.
Row 10 As row 4.
Rows 12, 14, 16 and 18 As row 2.
Repeat rows 1 to 18.

Six stitch cable

Materials Oiled wool, Aran-type or knitting worsted for an authentic nautical look; angora or mohair for wintry days.
Uses Jersey or jacket inset panel; all-over design for mother and daughter button-through cardigan.

Center panel of 10 sts.
Rows 1 and 3 (WS) K2, p6, k2.
Row 2 P2, k6, p2.
Row 4 P2, sl next 3 sts to cn and hold at back (or at front) ; k3, then k3 from cn, p2.
Rows 5 and 7 As rows 1 and 3.
Rows 6 and 8 As row 2.
Repeat rows 1 to 8.

Crossing cables

Materials Chunky or heavy-weight yarn for holiday cruising; angora or mohair for light-weight warmth.

Uses Inset panels for roomy, hooded sweater or child's sleeveless pullover; V-neck cardigan or snug-fitting hat or scarf.

Panel of 24 sts.

Note *Front Cross (FC) : sl 3 sts to cn and hold at front, k3, then k3 from cn.*
Back Cross (BC) : sl 3 sts to cn and hold at back, k3, then k3 from cn.
Single Front Cross (SFC) : sl 3 sts to cn and hold at front, p1, then k3 from cn.
Single Back Cross (SBC) : sl 1 st to cn and hold at back, k3, then p1 from cn.

Row 1 (WS) K2, p3, k4, p6, k4, p3, k2.
Row 2 P2, k3, p4, BC, p4, k3, p2.
Row 3 *and all subsequent WS rows.* Knit all knit sts and purl all purl sts.
Row 4 P2, (SFC, p2, SBC) twice, p2.
Row 6 P3, SFC, SBC, p2, SFC, SBC, p3.
Row 8 P4, FC, p4, BC, p4.
Row 10 P3, SBC, SFC, p2, SBC, SFC, p3.
Row 12 P2 (SBC, p2, SFC) twice, p2.
Row 14 P2, k3, p4, FC, p4, k3, p2.
Rows 16 and 18 Repeat rows 4 and 6.
Row 20 P4, BC, p4, FC, p4.
Rows 22 and 24 Repeat rows 10 and 12.
Repeat rows 1 to 24.

Banjo cable

Materials Middle to heavy-weight yarn for stitch clarity and a sporty effect.

Uses Single or double inset panel for man's button-through cardigan or sleeve detail on raglan sweater.

Center panel of 12 sts.

Row 1 (WS) K4, p4, k4.

Row 2 P4, k4, p4.

Row 3 K4, p1, sl 2 wyif, p1, k4.

Row 4 P2, sl next 3 sts to cn and hold at back, k1, then p1, k1, p1 from cn; sl next st to cn and hold at front, k1, p1, k1, then k1 from cn; p2.

Rows 5, 7 and 9 K2, (p1, k1) 3 times, p2, k2.

Rows 6, 8 and 10 P2, (k1, p1) 3 times, k2, p2.

Row 11 K2, sl 1 wyif, (k1, p1) 3 times, sl 1 wyif, k2.

Row 12 P2, sl next st to cn and hold at front, p2, k1, then k1 from cn; sl next 3 sts to cn and hold at back, k1, then k1, p2 from cn, p2.

Rows 13, 14, 15 and 16 Repeat rows 1 and 2 twice.

Repeat rows 1 to 16.

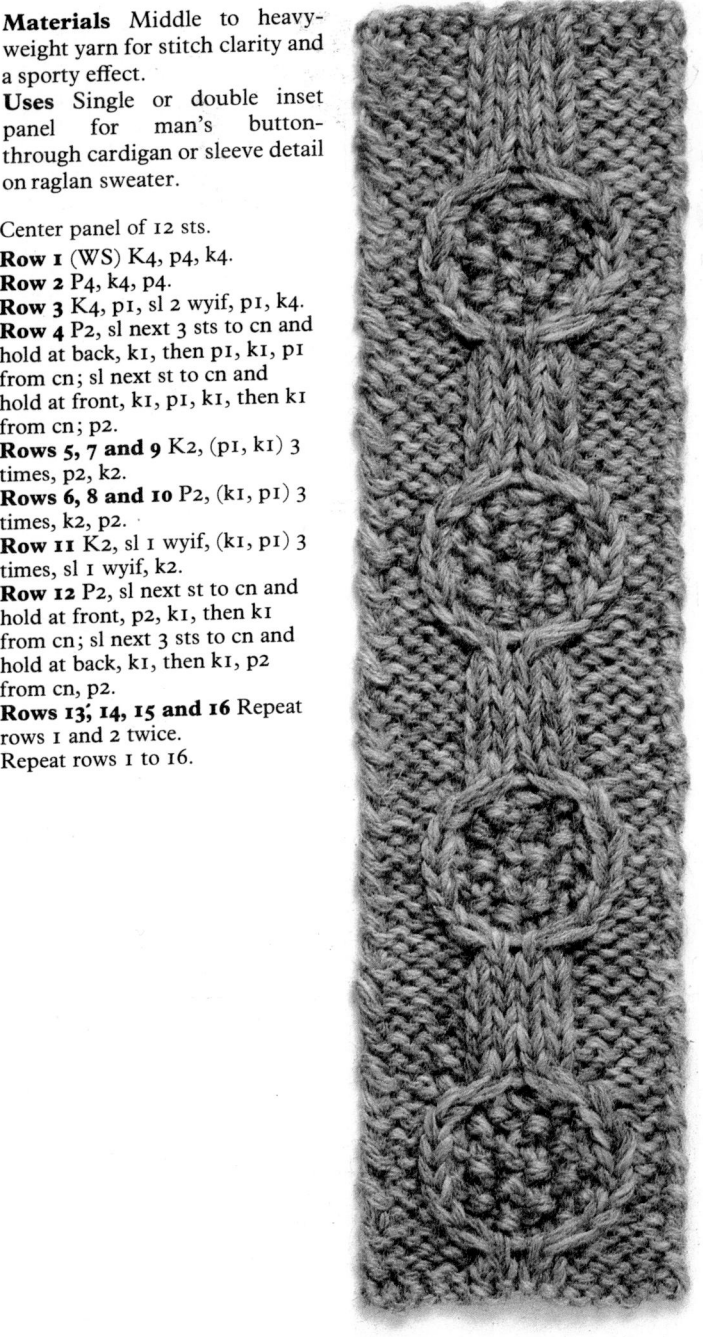

Patchwork cable

Materials Medium to heavy-weight yarn for a rich-textured, weatherproof fabric.

Uses All-over pattern for father and son jacket, hooded cape or traveling rug.

Multiple of 18 sts plus 1.

Note *Back Cross (BC) : sl 3 sts to cn and hold at back, k3, then k3 from cn.*

Row 1 (RS) K1, *p8, k1, p1, k6, p1, k1; rep from *.

Row 2 P1, *k1, p6, k1, p1, k8, p1; rep from *.

Row 3 K2, *p6, k2, p1, BC, p1, k2; rep from *, end last repeat k1.

Row 4 P1, *k1, p6, k1, p2, k6, p2; rep from *.

Row 5 K3, *p4, k3, p1, k6, p1, k3; rep from *, end last repeat k1.

Row 6 P1, *k1, p6, k1, p3, k4, p3; rep from *.

Row 7 K4, *p2, k4, p1, k6, p1, k4; rep from *, end last repeat K1.

Row 8 P1, *k1, p6, k1, p4, k2, p4; rep from *.

Row 9 *K10, p1, BC, p1; rep from *, end k1.

Rows 10 to 17 Repeat rows 8, 7, 6, 5, 4, 3, 2 and 1.

Row 18 P1, *k1, p6, k1, p1; rep from *.

Row 19 K1, *p1, k6, p1, k1, p8, k1; rep from *.

Row 20 P1, *k8, p1, k1, p6, k1, p1; rep from *.

Row 21 K1, *p1, BC, p1, k2, p6, k2; rep from *.

Row 22 P2, *k6, p2, k1, p6, k1, p2; rep from *, end last repeat p1.

Row 23 K1, *p1, k6, p1, k3, p4, k3; rep from *.

Row 24 P3, *k4, p3, k1, p6, k1, p3; rep from *, end last repeat p1.

Row 25 K1, *p1, k6, p1, k4, p2, k4; rep from *.

Row 26 P4, *k2, p4, k1, p6, k1, p4; rep from *, end last repeat p1.

Row 27 K1, *p1, BC, p1, k10; rep from *.

Rows 28 to 36 Repeat rows 26, 25, 24, 23, 22, 21, 20, 19 and 18. Repeat rows 1 to 36.

Bobble cable

Materials Aran-type yarn for an authentic fisherman style; tweedy wool for a sporty look.
Uses Double stripe for sweater inset panel, hat or scarf; single stripe for socks or mittens.

Center panel of 10 sts.
Row 1 (RS) (P2, k2) twice, p2.
Row 2 (K2, p2) twice, k2.
Row 3 P2, sl next 4 sts to cn and hold at front, k2, then sl the 2 purl sts from cn back to left-hand needle, then pass the cn with 2 remaining knit sts to back of work; p2 from left-hand needle, then k2 from cn; p2.
Rows 4, 6 and 8 Repeat row 2.
Rows 5, 7 and 9 Repeat row 1.
Row 10 Repeat row 2.
Repeat rows 1 to 10.

Double cable

Materials Medium to heavy-weight yarn for snug seaside holiday wear.
Uses All-over design for polo neck sweater, or combine with Aran patterns for sou'wester and cape or country-style coat.

Center panel of 12 sts.
Rows 1, 3, 5 and 7 (WS) K2, p8, k2.
Row 2 P2, sl next 2 sts to cn and hold at front, k2, then k2 from cn; sl next 2 sts to cn and hold at back, k2, then k2 from cn; p2.
Rows 4, 6 and 8 P2, k8, p2.
Repeat rows 1 to 8.

Framed cable

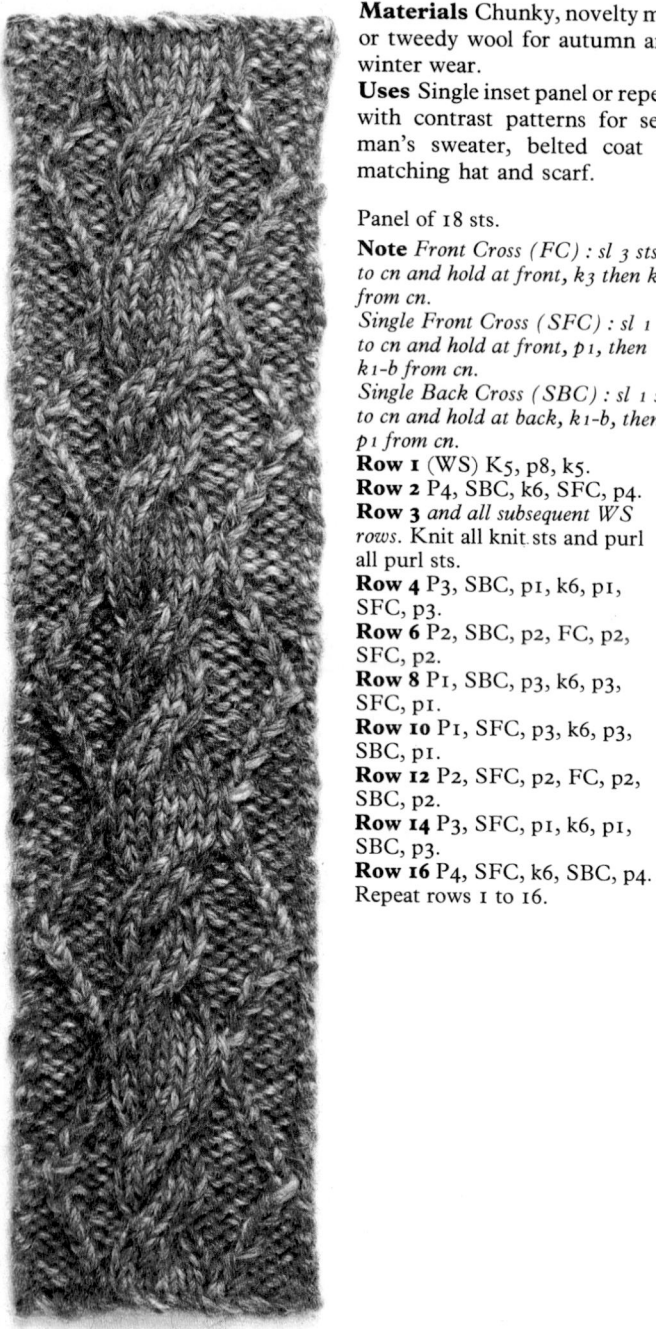

Materials Chunky, novelty mix or tweedy wool for autumn and winter wear.

Uses Single inset panel or repeat with contrast patterns for seaman's sweater, belted coat or matching hat and scarf.

Panel of 18 sts.

Note *Front Cross (FC) : sl 3 sts to cn and hold at front, k3 then k3 from cn.*
Single Front Cross (SFC) : sl 1 st to cn and hold at front, p1, then k1-b from cn.
Single Back Cross (SBC) : sl 1 st to cn and hold at back, k1-b, then p1 from cn.

Row 1 (WS) K5, p8, k5.
Row 2 P4, SBC, k6, SFC, p4.
Row 3 *and all subsequent WS rows.* Knit all knit sts and purl all purl sts.
Row 4 P3, SBC, p1, k6, p1, SFC, p3.
Row 6 P2, SBC, p2, FC, p2, SFC, p2.
Row 8 P1, SBC, p3, k6, p3, SFC, p1.
Row 10 P1, SFC, p3, k6, p3, SBC, p1.
Row 12 P2, SFC, p2, FC, p2, SBC, p2.
Row 14 P3, SFC, p1, k6, p1, SBC, p3.
Row 16 P4, SFC, k6, SBC, p4.
Repeat rows 1 to 16.

Aran lattice

Materials Lightly twisted knitting worsted yarn for warm, densely textured Arans; chunky yarn for furnishing.

Uses Sweater inset panel, or combine with other Aran patterns for classic fisherman's jersey or girl's poncho and hat; cushion set panel.

Multiple of 6 sts plus 2.

Rows 1 and 3 (WS) K1, *k2, p4; rep from *, end k1.

Row 2 K1, *sl next 2 sts to cn and hold at front, k2, then k2 from cn; p2; rep from *, end k1.

Row 4 K1, p2, *k2, sl next 2 sts to cn and hold at back, k2, then p2 from cn; rep from *, end k5.

Rows 5 and 7 K1, *p4, k2; rep from *, end k1.

Row 6 K1, *p2, sl next 2 sts to cn and hold at back, k2, then k2 from cn; rep from *, end k1.

Row 8 K5, *sl next 2 sts to cn and hold at front, p2, then k2 from cn, k2; rep from *, end p2, k1.

Repeat rows 1 to 8.

Tudor grillwork

Materials Knitting worsted or tweedy wool for a warm, sculptured fabric; Shetland 4-ply wool or mohair for comfort.
Uses Father and son blouson jacket or sweater inset panel; overall design for classic V-neck cardigan or slipover.

Multiple of 10 sts plus 2.

Note *Front Cross (FC) : sl 2 sts to dpn and hold in front, p2, then k2 from dpn.*
Back Cross (BC) : sl 2 sts to dpn and hold in back, k2, then p2 from dpn.
Back Knit Cross (BKC) : sl 2 sts to dpn and hold in back, k2, then k2 from dpn.
Rows 1, 3, 5 and 7 (RS) P5, *RT, p8; rep from *, end RT, p5.
Rows 2, 4 and 6 K5, *p2, k8; rep from *, end p2, k5.
Row 8 K5, * purl into the front and back of each of the next 2 sts, k8; rep from *, end last repeat k5.
Row 9 P5, *BKC, p8; rep from *, end last repeat p5.
Row 10 K5, *p4, k8; rep from *, end p4, k5.
Row 11 P3, *BC, FC, p4; rep from *, end last repeat p3.
Row 12 K3, *p2, k4; rep from *, end p2, k3.
Row 13 P1, *BC, p4, FC; rep from *, end p1.
Row 14 K1, p2, *k8, p4; rep from *, end k8, p2, k1.
Row 15 P1, k2, *p8, BKC; rep from *, end p8, k2, p1.
Rows 16 and 18 Repeat rows 14 and 12.
Row 17 P1, *FC, p4, BC; rep from *, end p1.
Row 19 P3, *FC, BC, p4; rep from *, end last repeat p3.
Row 20 K5, *(p2 tog) twice, k8; rep from *, end last repeat k5.
Repeat rows 1 to 20.

Leaf rib

Materials Lightly twisted knitting worsted wool for a fisherman look; chunky or tweedy yarn for furnishing.
Uses Guernsey yoke or inset panel, all-over design for slipover; center panel for bedspread or floor cushion.

Multiple of 16 sts plus 1.

Note *Right Twist (RT) : K 2 tog, leaving sts on left needle. Insert right needle from the front between the two sts knitted together. Knit the first st again, then slip both sts from needle together.*
Left Twist (LT) : With right needle behind left needle, miss one st and knit second st through the back. Insert right needle into backs of both the missed st and the second st, and k 2 tog-b.
Row 1 *(WS) and all other WS rows.* Purl.
Row 2 K1, *LT, (RT) twice, k3, (LT) twice, RT, k1; rep from *.
Row 4 K2, *LT, (RT) twice, k1, (LT) twice, RT, k3; rep from *, end last repeat k2.

Row 6 K1, *(LT) twice, RT, k3, LT, (RT) twice, k1; rep from *.
Row 8 K2, *(LT) twice, RT, k1, LT, (RT) twice, k3; rep from *, end last repeat k2.
Row 10 K1, *(LT) 3 times, k3, (RT) 3 times, k1; rep from *.
Row 12 K2, *(LT) 3 times, k1, (RT) 3 times, k3; rep from *, end last repeat k2.
Rows 14, 16, 18, 20 and 22
Repeat rows 10, 8, 6, 4 and 2.
Row 24 K2, *(LT) 3 times, k1, (LT) 3 times, k3; rep from *, end last repeat k2.
Row 26 K1, *(RT) 3 times, k3, (LT) 3 times, k1; rep from *.
Row 28 Repeat row 24.
Repeat rows 1 to 28.

Lattice cable

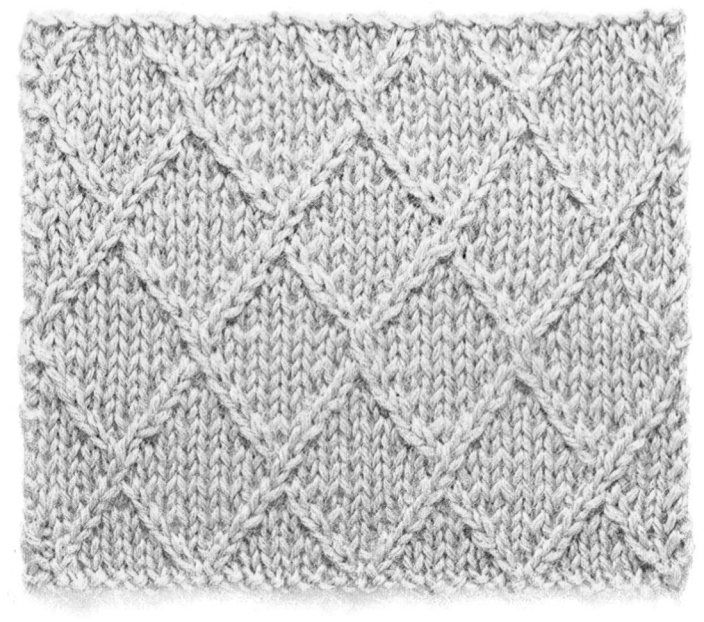

Materials Shetland 4-ply, medium-weight wool or novelty mix for town and country wear; angora or poodle for luxury.

Uses Smock or sweater yoke, inset panel or sleeve band; all-over design for classic-style sweater or baby's crib cover.

Multiple of 8 sts plus 2.

Row 1 *(WS) and all other WS rows.* Purl.

Row 2 K1, *LT, k4, RT; rep from *, end k1.

Row 4 K2, *LT, k2, RT, k2; rep from *.

Row 6 K3, *LT, RT, k4; rep from *, end last repeat k3.

Row 8 K4, *RT, k6; rep from *, end last repeat k4.

Row 10 K3, *RT, LT, k4; rep from *, end last repeat k3.

Row 12 K2, *RT, k2, LT, k2; rep from *.

Row 14 K1, *RT, k4, LT; rep from *, end k1.

Row 16 K8, *LT, k6; rep from *, end k2.

Repeat row 1 to 16.

For LT and RT see p39.

COLORSLIP

Colorslip patterns are made by knitting some stitches and slipping others (see p13). It is one of the easiest methods of introducing stitch texture into two-color or multi-color work. Such patterns look colorful and intricate but are quick and easy to knit. Patterns include tweeds, classic colored stripes and chevrons through interlaced bands to basketweave.

Chevron stripes

Materials 4-ply, knitting worsted or acrylic yarn for a bright, sporty effect; loosely twisted chunky yarn for a bolder look.
Uses Sweater yoke or inset panel; mix with other pattern bands across man's vest front or blouson jacket.

Multiple of 4 sts.
Colours A, B and C.
Cast on with A and purl one row.
Row 1 (RS) with B, *k1, sl 3 wyib; rep from *.
Row 2 With B, *p1, sl 1 wyif, p3; rep from *, end sl 1, p2.
Row 3 With B, knit.
Row 4 With B, purl.
Rows 5 to 8 With C, repeat rows 1 to 4.
Rows 9 to 12 With A, repeat rows 1 to 4.
Repeat rows 1 to 12.

Greek tile

Materials Smooth, medium-weight yarn for color contrast; poodle or mohair for a softer image.
Uses Man's classic style V-neck slipover or child's hat; sweater yoke and inset sleeve band.

Multiple of 10 sts plus 2.

Colors A and B.

Note *On all RS (odd-numbered) rows slip all sl sts wyib; on all WS (even-numbered) rows slip all sl sts wyif.*

Row 1 (RS) With A, knit.
Row 2 With A, purl.
Row 3 With B, k1, *k8, sl 2; rep from *, end k1.
Row 4 *and all subsequent WS rows.* Using the same color as previous row, purl across, slipping wyif all slipped sts on previous row.
Row 5 With A, k1, *sl 2, k4, sl 2, k2; rep from *, end k1.

Row 7 With B, k1, *k2, sl 2, k4, sl 2; rep from *, end k1.
Row 9 With A, k1, *sl 2, k8; rep from *, end k1.
Row 11 With B, knit.
Row 13 With A, *k4, sl 2, k4; rep from *, end k2..
Row 15 With B, k2, *sl 2, k2, sl 2, k4; rep from *.
Row 17 With A, *k4, sl 2, k2, sl 2; rep from *, end k2.
Row 19 With B, *k6, sl 2, k2; rep from *, end k2.
Row 20 See row 4.
Repeat rows 1 to 20.

Windowpane

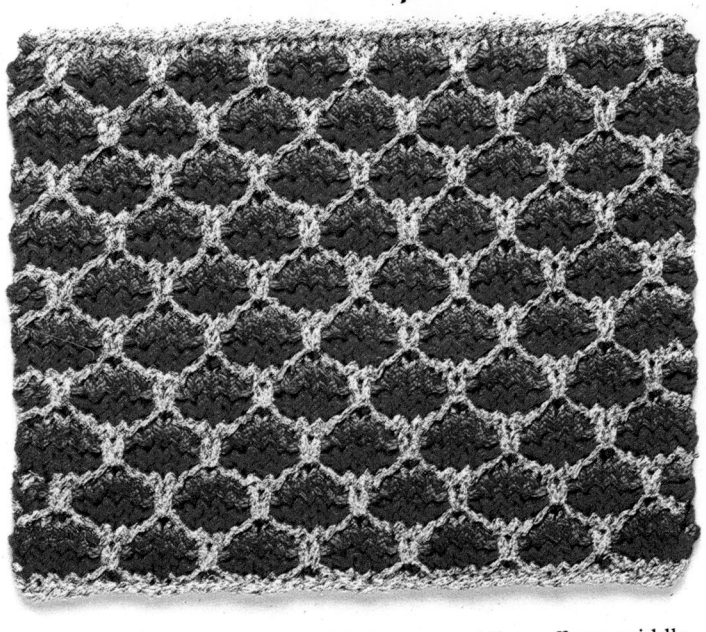

Materials Lurex, rayon or silk for a sparkling effect; middle-weight yarn for a rich-textured fabric.
Uses Inset panel for evening waistcoat, belt or purse; all-over pattern for toddler's jacket and matching hat.

Multiple of 6 sts plus 5.

Colors A, B and C.

Row 1 (WS) With A, p4, *sl 3 wyib, p3; rep from *, end p1.

Row 2 With B, knit.

Row 3 With B, repeat row 1.

Rows 4 and 5 With C, repeat rows 2 and 3.

Row 6 With A, k5, *insert needle from front under the 3 loose strands and upward to knit next st, catching all 3 strands behind st as it is knitted; k5; rep from *.

Row 7 With A, p1, *sl 3 wyib, p3; rep from *, end last repeat p1.

Row 8 With B, knit.

Row 9 With B, repeat row 7.

Rows 10 and 11 With C, repeat rows 8 and 9.

Row 12 With A, k2, rep from * of row 6; end last repeat k2 instead of k5.

Repeat rows 1 to 12.

Variegated check

Materials Cotton yarn and lurex for a glittery effect; 4-ply crêpe or acrylic yarn for a sporty look.

Uses Border design for mother and daughter loose-fitting jacket; golf cardigan inset panel.

Multiple of 22 sts plus 1.

Colors A and B.

Note *on the RS (odd-numbered) rows sl all sl sts wyib; on WS (even-numbered) rows sl all sl sts wyif.*

Row 1 (RS) With A, knit.

Row 2 With A, purl.

Row 3 With B, k1, *sl 3, k2, sl 2, k3, sl 1, k3, sl 2, k2, sl 3, k1; rep from *.

Row 4 With B, p1, *sl 3, p2, sl 2, p3, sl 1, p3, sl 2, p2, sl 3, p1; rep from *.

Row 5 With A, k1, *k3, sl 2, k2, sl 3, k1, sl 3, k2, sl 2, k3, sl 1; rep from *, end last repeat k1 instead of sl 1.

Row 6 With A, p1, *p3, sl 2, p2, sl 3, p1, sl 3, p2, sl 2, p3, sl 1; rep from *, end last repeat p1 instead of sl 1.

Rows 7 to 14 Repeat rows 3 to 6 twice more.

Row 15 With A, knit.

Row 16 With A, purl.

Rows 17 and 18 With B, repeat rows 5 and 6.

Rows 19 and 20 With A, repeat rows 3 and 4.

Rows 21 to 28 Repeat rows 17 to 20 twice more.

Repeat rows 1 to 28.

Coral sand

Materials Use double-ended needles with 4-ply wool and lurex for an extra special effect; plain, medium-weight yarn for a sporty look.
Uses Inset panel for mother and daughter classic-style sweater; all-over pattern for hooded blouson jacket or scarf border.

Multiple of 10 sts plus 5.
Colors A and B
Row 1 (WS) With A, purl.
Row 2 With B, knit. Sl sts to other end of dpn.
Row 3 With A, knit.
Row 4 With B, p1, *sl 3 wyif, p7; rep from *, end sl 3, p1. Sl sts to other end of dpn.
Row 5 With A, purl.
Row 6 With B, k1, *sl 3 wyib, k7; rep from *, end sl 3, k1. Sl sts to other end of needle.
Row 7 With A, knit.
Row 8 With B, repeat row 4. Sl sts to other end of needle.
Rows 9, 10 and 11 Repeat rows 1, 2 and 3.
Row 12 With B, p6, *sl 3 wyif, p7; rep from *, end sl 3, p6. Sl sts to other end of needle.
Row 13 With A, purl.
Row 14 With B, k6, *sl 3 wyib, k7; rep from *, end sl 3, k6. Sl sts to other end of needle.
Row 15 With A, knit.
Row 16 With B, repeat row 12. Sl sts to other end of needle.
Repeat rows 1 to 16.

Yang and yin

Materials Smooth twisted yarn for a classic look; chunky yarn in contrasting colors for a bold effect.
Uses All-over repeat for father and son sweater, cushion set, rug or blanket border.

Multiple of 20 sts plus 2.
Colors A and B.
Note *On all RS rows, sl all sl-sts with yarn in* back.
Cast on with A and purl one row.
Row 1 (RS) With B, k1, *k2, sl 2, k6, sl 2, k8; rep from *, end k1.
Row 2 and all other WS rows. Purl the same sts worked on previous row, with the same color; sl st all the same sl-sts with yarn in front.
Row 3 With A, k1, *k4, (sl 2, k6) twice; rep from *, end k1.
Row 5 With B, k1, *sl 2, k4, sl 2, k2; rep from *, end k1.
Row 7 With A, k1, *k2, (sl 2, k4) 3 times; rep from *, end k1.
Row 9 With B, k1, *k4, sl 2, k6,

sl 2, k4, sl 2; rep from *, end k1.
Row 11 With A, k1, * sl 2, k4, sl 2, k2; rep from *, end k1.
Row 13 With B, k1, *k2, sl 2, k10, sl 2, k4; rep from *, end k1.
Row 15 With A, k1, *sl 2, k10, sl 2, k6; rep from *, end k1.
Row 17 With B, k1, *k4, sl 2, k2, sl 2; rep from *, end k1.
Row 19 With A, k1, *k2, sl 2, k6, sl 2, k4, sl 2, k2; rep from *, end k1.
Row 21 With B, k1, *(sl 2, k4) twice, sl 2, k6; rep from *, end k1.
Row 23 With A, k1, *k4, sl 2, k2, sl 2; rep from *, end k1.
Row 24 See row 2.
Repeat rows 1 to 24.

Florentine

Materials Medium-weight wool, double crêpe or rayon for a figure-flattering effect; rug wool for wear.

Uses All-over pattern for mother and daughter short jacket, skirt and matching scarf; sofa upholstery or floor cushion.

Multiple of 24 sts plus 2.

Colors A and B.

Note *On all RS (odd-numbered) rows all sl sts are slipped wyib. On WS (even-numbered) rows all sl sts are slipped wyif.*

Cast on with A and purl one row.

Row 1 (RS) With B, k1, *sl 1, k2; rep from *, end k1.

Row 2 With B, k1, *p2, sl 1; rep from *, end k1.

Row 3 With A, k1, *k1, sl 1, (k2, sl 1) 3 times, k3, (sl 1, k2) 3 times, sl 1; rep from *, end k1.

Row 4 With A, k1, *sl 1, (p2, sl 1) 3 times, p3, (sl 1, p2) 3 times, sl 1, p1; rep from *, end k1.

Row 5 With B, k1, *k2, (sl 1, k2) 3 times, sl 1, k1, sl 1, (k2, sl 1) 3 times, k1; rep from *, end k1.

Row 6 With B, k1, *p1, (sl 1, p2) 3 times, sl 1, p1, sl 1, (p2, sl 1) 3 times, p2; rep from *, end k1.

Rows 7 and 8 With A, repeat rows 1 and 2.

Rows 9 and 10 With B, repeat rows 3 and 4.

Rows 11 and 12 With A, repeat rows 5 and 6.

Repeat rows 1 to 12.

Sporting check

Materials Knitting worsted or random-dyed yarn for a basketweave texture.

Uses All-over pattern for father and son polo neck sweater, man's classic-style cardigan or bath mat.

Multiple of 10 sts plus 2.

Colors A and B.

Row 1 (RS) With A, knit.

Row 2 With A, (k1, p1) twice, k1, *p2, k1, p1, k1; rep from *, end p2.

Row 3 With B, k1, *k5, (sl 1 wyib, k1), twice, sl 1 wyib; rep from *, end k1.

Row 4 With B, k1, *(sl 1 wyif, k1) twice, sl 1 wyif, k5; rep from *, end k1.

Row 5 With A, knit.

Row 6 With A, k1, *(p1, k1) twice, p1, k5; rep from *, end k1.

Rows 7, 8, 9, 10, 11 and 12 Repeat rows 3, 4, 5 and 6, then rows 3 and 4 again.

Rows 13 and 14 With A, repeat rows 1 and 2.

Row 15 With B, k1, *(sl 1 wyib, k1) twice, sl 1 wyib, k5; rep from *, end k1.

Row 16 With B, k1, *k5, (sl 1 wyif, k1) twice, sl 1 wyif; rep from *, end k1.

Row 17 With A, knit.

Row 18 With A, k1, *k5, (p1, k1) twice, p1; rep from *, end k1

Rows 19, 20, 21, 22, 23 and 24 Repeat rows 15, 16, 17 and 18, then rows 15 and 16 again.

Repeat rows 1 to 24.

Interlacing stripe

Materials Knitting worsted, crêpe or tweedy wool for extra warmth; heavy or chunky yarn for classic-style furnishing.

Uses Jacket or sweater inset panel or horizontal band; rug border design, cushion set or blanket.

Multiple of 16 sts plus 3.

Colors A and B.

Note *On RS rows, sl all sl sts wyib.*

Cast on with A and knit one row.

Row 1 (RS) With B, k1, *(k1, sl 1, k3, sl 1) twice, k3, sl 1; rep from *, end k2.

Row 2 *and all WS rows.* Knit all sts worked on previous row, with same color; sl all same sl sts wyif.

Row 3 With A, k1, *sl 1, k3; rep from *, end sl 1, k1.

Row 5 With B, k4, *sl 1, k1, (sl 1, k3) twice, sl 1, k5; rep from *, end last repeat k4.

Row 7 With A, k2, *sl 2, k3, (sl 1, k3) twice, sl 2, k1; rep from *, end k1.

Row 9 With B, k4, *(sl 1, k3) twice, sl 1, k1, sl 1, k5; rep from *, end last repeat k4.

Row 11 With A, repeat row 3.

Row 13 With B, k2, *(sl 1, k3) twice, sl 1, k1, sl 1, k3, sl 1, k1;

rep from *, end k1.

Row 15 With A, k3, *sl 1, k3; rep from *.

Row 17 With B, k2, *(sl 1, k1, sl 1, k3) twice, sl 1, k3; rep from *, end k1.

Row 19 With A, repeat row 3.

Row 21 With B, k4, *sl 1, k1, sl 1, k5, (sl 1, k3) twice; rep from *, end last repeat k2.

Row 23 With A, k3, *sl 1, k3, sl 2, k1, sl 2, k3, sl 1, k3; rep from *.

Row 25 With B, k2, *sl 1, k3, sl 1, k5, sl 1, k1, sl 1, k3; rep from *, end k1.

Row 27 With A, repeat row 3.

Row 29 With B, k4, *(sl 1, k3, sl 1, k1) twice, sl 1, k3; rep from *, end last repeat k2.

Row 31 With A, repeat row 15.

Row 32 See row 2.

Repeat rows 1 to 32.

Rainbow zigzag

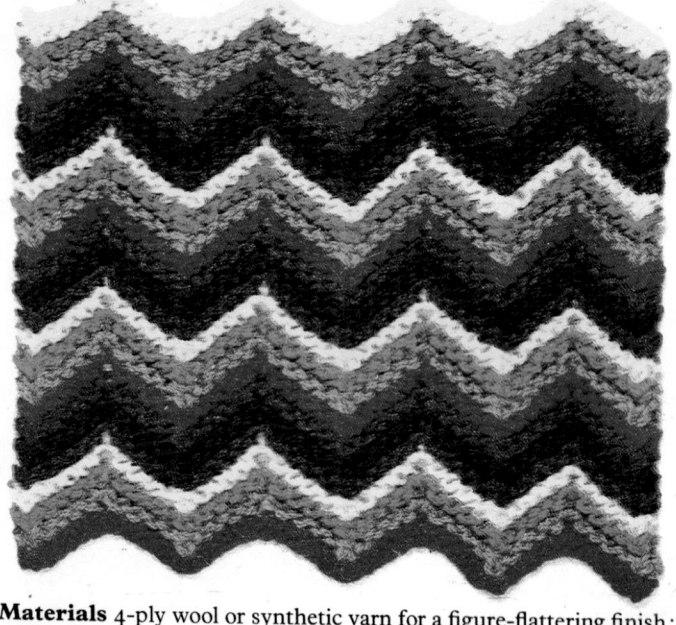

Materials 4-ply wool or synthetic yarn for a figure-flattering finish; chunky yarn for furnishing.

Uses All-over pattern for matching jacket, skirt and scarf or sleeveless slipover; bed cover or cushion set.

Multiple of 12 sts plus 3.

Colors A and B.

Cast on with A and knit one row.

Row 1 (RS) With B, k1, sl 1, k1, psso, *k9, sl 2, k1, p2sso; rep from *, end k9, k2 tog, k1.

Row 2 With B, k1, *p1, k4 (k1, yo, k1) in next st, k4; rep from *, end p1, k1.

Rows 3 and 4 With A, repeat rows 1 and 2.

Repeat rows 1 to 4.

BOBBLE & EMBOSSED

Deeply textured bobble and embossed patterns are created by raising and lowering the surface of the knitting. This is done by increasing repeatedly into the same stitch, to form a round or flat cluster of stitches and then decreasing the cluster according to your particular pattern. This group of stitch patterns offers one of the widest ranges of surface decoration and texture, from small berry-like repeats to flowing vine, bead and bouquet patterns.

Gooseberry stitch

Materials Oiled or knitting worsted wool for a traditional Aran look; baby wool for nursery wear.

Uses Mix panel with Aran patterns for fisherman's jersey; all-over design for baby's carriage set or shawl.

Odd number of sts.

Row 1 (RS) Knit.
Row 2 K1, *(p1, yo, p1, yo, p1) in next st, making 5 sts from one; k1, rep from *.
Row 3 Purl.
Row 4 K1, *sl 2 wyif, p3 tog, p2sso, k1; rep from *.
Row 5 Knit.
Row 6 K2, *(p1, yo, p1, yo, p1) in next st, k1; rep from *, end k1.
Row 7 Purl.
Row 8 K2, *sl 2 wyif, p3 tog, p2sso, k1; rep from *, end k1.
Repeat rows 1 to 8.

Bluebell pattern

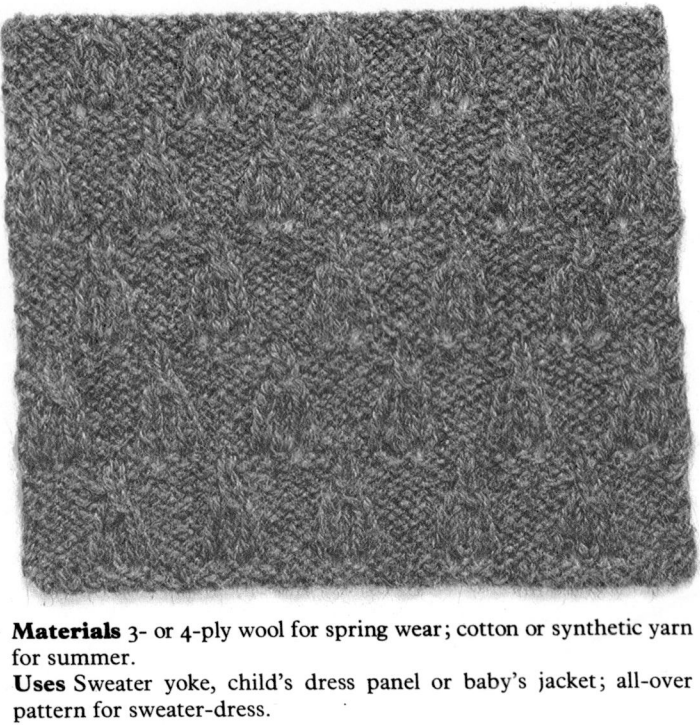

Materials 3- or 4-ply wool for spring wear; cotton or synthetic yarn for summer.

Uses Sweater yoke, child's dress panel or baby's jacket; all-over pattern for sweater-dress.

Multiple of 6 sts plus 5.

Row 1 (RS) P2, *k1, p5; rep from *, end k1, p2.

Row 2 K2, *p1, k5; rep from *, end p1, k2.

Row 3 P5, *yo, k1, yo, p5; rep from *.

Rows 4, 6 and 8 K5, *p3, k5; rep from *.

Rows 5 and 7 P5, *k3, p5; rep from *.

Row 9 P5, *sl 1, k2 tog, psso, p5; rep from *.

Rows 10 and 12 K5, *p1, k5; rep from *.

Row 11 P5, *k1, p5; rep from *.

Row 13 P2, *yo, k1, yo, p5; rep from *, end yo, k1, yo, p2.

Rows 14, 16 and 18 K2, *p3, k5; rep from *, end p3, k2.

Rows 15 and 17 P2, *k3, p5; rep from *, end k3, p2.

Row 19 P2, *sl 1, k2 tog, psso, p5; rep from *, end sl 1, k2 tog, psso, p2.

Row 20 Repeat row 2.

Repeat rows 1 to 20.

Berry stitch

Materials Thick or medium-weight wool for a fisherman look; 4-ply wool or acrylic mix for everyday wear.
Uses Sweater inset panel or alternate with cables for Arans; all-over design for mother and daughter cardigan.

Multiple of 4 sts.
Row 1 (WS) *(K1, yo, k1) in same st, p3 tog; rep from *.
Row 2 *K1, p3; rep from *.
Row 3 *K3, p1; rep from *.
Row 4 *P1, k3; rep from *.
Row 5 *P3 tog, (k1, yo, k1) in same st; rep from *.
Row 6 *P3, k1; rep from *.
Row 7 *P1, k3; rep from *.
Row 8 *K3, p1; rep from *.
Repeat rows 1 to 8.

Puffball pattern

Materials Thick, medium-weight wool or novelty mix for outdoor wear; angora or mohair for light-weight warmth.
Uses Fisherman's sweater inset panel; all-over pattern for slip-over or V-neck button-through cardigan.

Multiple of 10 sts plus 2.
Rows 1 and 3 (WS) Purl.
Row 2 Knit.
Row 4 K1, *(k5, turn, p5, turn) 3 times, k10; rep from *, end k1.
Rows 5, 6 and 7 Repeat rows 1, 2 and 3.
Row 8 K6, rep from * of row 4; end last repeat k6 instead of k10.
Repeat rows 1 to 8.

Twining vine pattern

Materials Medium-weight yarn for lightly embossed town or country classics; angora or poodle for softness.
Uses Inset front panel for twinset, loose-fitting cardigan or jacket; all-over repeat for overblouse or shawl.

Center panel of 26 sts.

Row 1 (WS) K12, p5, k4, p3, k16.
Row 2 P14, p2 tog, knit into front and back of next st, k2, p4, k2, yo, k1, yo, k2, p12.
Row 3 K12, p7, k4, p2, k1, p1, k15.
Row 4 P13, p2 tog, k1, purl into front and back of next st (purl inc), k2, p4, k3, yo, k1, yo, k3, p12.
Row 5 K12, p9, k4, p2, k2, p1, k16.
Row 6 P12, p2 tog, k1, purl inc, p1, k2, p4, sl 1, k1, psso, k5, k2 tog, p12.
Row 7 K12, p7, k4, p2, k3, p1, k13.
Row 8 P11, p2 tog, k1, purl inc, p2, k2, p4, sl 1, k1, psso, k3, k2 tog, p12.
Row 9 K12, p5, k4, p2, k4, p1, k12.
Row 10 P12, yo, k1, yo, p4, k2, p4, sl 1, k1, psso, k1, k2 tog, p12.
Row 11 K12, p3, k4, p2, k4, p3, k12.
Row 12 P12, (k1, yo) twice, k1, p4, k1, knit into the *back* of running thread (M1), k1, p2 tog, p2, sl 2 k-wise, k1, p2sso, p12.
Row 13 K16, p3, k4, p5, k12.

Row 14 P12, k2, yo, k1, yo, k2, p4, k1, knit into front and back of next st, k1, p2 tog, p14.
Row 15 K15, p1, k1, p2, k4, p7, k12.
Row 16 P12, k3, yo, k1, yo, k3, p4, k2, purl inc, k1, p2 tog, p13.
Row 17 K14, p1, k2, p2, k4, p9, k12.
Row 18 P12, sl 1, k1, psso, k5, k2 tog, p4, k2, p1, purl inc, k1, p2 tog, p12.
Row 19 K13, p1, k3, p2, k4, p7, k12.
Row 20 P12, sl 1, k1, psso, k3, k2 tog, p4, k2, p2, purl inc, k1, p2 tog, p11.
Row 21 K12, p1, k4, p2, k4, p5, k12.
Row 22 P12, sl 1, k1, psso, k1, k2 tog, p4, k2, p4, yo, k1, yo, p12.
Row 23 K12, p3, k4, p2, k4, p3, k12.
Row 24 P12, sl 2 k-wise, k1, p2sso, p2, p2 tog, k1, M1, k1, p4, (k1, yo) twice, k1, p12.
Repeat rows 1 to 24.

Grape pattern

Materials 3- or 4-ply or knitting worsted yarn for country fair wear.
Uses Cardigan inset panel or shawl border; all-over design for sleeveless pullover.

Multiple of 20 sts plus 1.

Note *Throughout pattern MB (Make Bobble) as follows: (k1, yo, k1, yo, k1) into the same st forming 5 bobble sts; turn work around and p5 across the bobble sts; turn again and k5, then pass the 4th, 3rd, 2nd, and first sts separately over the last st knitted, completing bobble.*

Row 1 (RS) K1, *(p4, k1) twice, p4, MB, p4, k1; rep from *.
Row 2 P1, *k4, pl-b (into bobble st); (k4, p1) 3 times; rep from *.
Row 3 K1, *(p4, k1) twice, p3, MB, p1, MB, p3, k1; rep from *.
Row 4 P1, *k3, pl-b, k1, pl-b, k3, p1, (k4, p1) twice; rep from *.
Row 5 K1, *(p4, k1) twice, p2, MB, (p1, MB) twice, p2, k1; rep from *.

Row 6 P1, *k2, pl-b, (k1, pl-b) twice, k2, p1, (k4, p1) twice; rep from *.
Row 7 K1, *p4, MB, (p4, k1) 3 times; rep from *.
Row 8 P1, *(k4, p1) twice, k4, pl-b, k4, p1; rep from *.
Row 9 K1, *p3, MB, p1, MB, p3, k1, (p4, k1) twice; rep from *.
Row 10 P1, *(k4, p1) twice, k3, pl-b, k1, pl-b, k3, p1; rep from *.
Row 11 K1, *p2, MB, (pl, MB) twice, p2, k1, (p4, k1) twice; rep from *.
Row 12 P1, *(k4, p1) twice, k2, (pl-b, k1) twice, pl-b, k2, pl; rep from *.
Repeat rows 1 to 12.

Bouquet stitch

Materials Medium-weight yarn for a deep-textured fabric; chunky or knitting worsted for a more sculptured look.

Uses Inset panel for sweater, cardigan or socks; cushion or bedspread border.

Panel of 16 sts.

Note *Front Cross (FC) : sl 1 st to cn and hold in front ; p 1, then k 1 from cn.*
Front Knit Cross (FKC) : same as FC but knit both sts.
Back Cross (BC) : sl 1 st to cn and hold at back, k 1, then p 1 from cn.
Back Knit Cross (BKC) : same as BC, but knit both sts.

Row 1 (WS) K7, p2, k7.
Row 2 P6, BKC, FKC, p6.
Row 3 K5, FC, p2, BC, k5.
Row 4 P4, BC, BKC, FKC, FC, p4.
Row 5 K3, FC, k1, p4, k1, BC, k3.
Row 6 P2, BC, p1, BC, k2, FC, p1, FC, p2.
Row 7 (K2, p1) twice, k1, p2, k1, (p1, k2) twice.
Row 8 P2, Make Bobble (MB) as follows : (k1, p1) twice into next st, turn and p4, turn and k4, turn and (p2 tog) twice, turn and k2 tog, completing bobble; p1, BC, p1, k2, p1, FC, p1, MB, p2.
Row 9 K4, p1, k2, p2, k2, p1, k4.
Row 10 P4, MB, p2, k2, p2, MB, p4.
Repeat rows 1 to 10.

Bead pattern

Materials 4-ply crêpe, novelty mix or acrylic yarn for a summery look; knitting worsted yarn or mohair for warmth.

Uses Dress yoke or inset panel; all-over design for slipover, vest or cardigan front.

Multiple of 10 sts plus 4.

Row 1 (RS) P4, *k1, p4, yo, k1, yo, p4; rep from *.

Row 2 K4, *yo, p3, yo, k4, p1, k4; rep from *.

Row 3 P4, *k1, p4, yo, k5, yo, p4; rep from *.

Row 4 K4, *yo, p7, yo, k4, p1, k4; rep from *.

Row 5 P4, *k1, p4, yo, k9, yo, p4; rep from *.

Row 6 K4, *p2 tog, p7, p2 tog-b, k4, p1, k4, rep from *.

Row 7 P4, *k1, p4, sl 1, k1, psso, k5, k2 tog, p4; rep from *.

Row 8 K4, *p2 tog, p3, p2 tog-b, k4, p1, k4; rep from *.

Row 9 P4, *k1, p4, sl 1, k1, psso, k1, k2 tog, p4; rep from *.

Row 10 K4, *p3 tog, k4, p1, k4; rep from *.

Row 11 P4, *yo, k1, yo, p4, k1, p4; rep from *.

Row 12 K4, *p1, k4, yo, p3, yo, k4; rep from *.

Row 13 P4, *yo, k5, yo, p4, k1, p4; rep from *.

Row 14 K4, *p1, k4, yo, p7, yo, k4; rep from *.

Row 15 P4, *yo, k9, yo, p4, k1, p4, rep from *.

Row 16 K4, *p1, k4, p2 tog, p7, p2 tog-b, k4; rep from *.

Row 17 P4, *sl 1, k1, psso, k5, k2 tog, p4, k1, p4; rep from *.

Row 18 K4, *p1, k4, p2 tog, p3, p2, tog-b, k4; rep from *.

Row 19 P4, *sl 1, k1, psso, k1, k2 tog, p4, k1, p4; rep from *.

Row 20 K4, *p1, k4, p3 tog, k4; rep from *.

Repeat rows 1 to 20.

Sheaf stitch

Materials 3- or 4-ply yarn, crêpe or knitting worsted wool for a deep-textured fabric with a young look.
Uses Mother and daughter sweater or coat yoke, toddler's tops or baby's crib cover.

Multiple of 8 sts plus 2.

Rows 1 and 3 (WS) K2, *p2, k2; rep from *.

Row 2 P2, *k2, p2; rep from *.

Row 4 P2, *insert right needle from front between 6th and 7th sts on left needle and draw through a loop; sl this loop onto left needle and knit it together with first st on left needle; k1, p2, k2, p2; rep from *.

Rows 5 and 7 Repeat rows 1 and 3.

Row 6 Repeat row 2.

Row 8 P2, k2, p2, *draw loop from between 6th and 7th sts as before and knit together with first st, then k1, p2, k2, p2; rep from *, end k2, p2.
Repeat rows 1 to 8.

Bobble and diamond cable

Materials Medium-weight wool, crêpe or acrylic for a rich-textured sporty look.

Uses Inset panel for jerseys in all sizes or socks and mitts for the family; all-over repeat for pullover.

Panel of 17 sts.

Note *Front Cross (FC) : sl 2 sts to cn and hold at front, p1 then k2 from cn.*

Back Cross (BC) : sl 1 st to cn and hold at back, k2, then p1 from cn.

Rows 1 and 3 (WS) K6, p2, k1, p2, k6.

Row 2 P6, sl next 3 sts to cn and hold at back, k2, then sl the purl st from cn back to left needle and purl it, then k2 from cn; p6.

Row 4 P5, BC, k1, FC, p5.

Row 5 *and all subsequent WS rows.* Knit all knit sts and purl all purl sts.

Row 6 P4, BC, k1, p1, k1, FC, p4.

Row 8 P3, BC, (k1, p1) twice, k1, FC, p3.

Row 10 P2, BC, (k1, p1) 3 times, k1, FC, p2.

Row 12 P2, FC, (p1, k1) 3 times, p1, BC, p2.

Row 14 P3, FC, (p1, k1) twice, p1, BC, p3.

Row 16 P4, FC, p1, k1, p1, BC, p4.

Row 18 P5, FC, p1, BC, p5.

Row 20 Repeat row 2.

Row 22 P5, BC, p1, FC, p5.

Row 24 P4, BC, p3, FC, p4.

Row 26 P4, k2, p2. Make Bobble as follows : (k1, yo, k1, yo, k1) in next st, turn and p5, turn and k5, turn and p2 tog, p1, p2 tog, turn and sl 1, k2 tog, psso, completing bobble; p2, k2, p4.

Row 28 P4, FC, p3, BC, p4.

Row 30 Repeat row 18.

Repeat rows 1 to 30.

Tassel pattern

Materials Soft, lightly twisted chunky to 4-ply yarn for a raised bobble effect.

Uses Inset vertical panels for party cardigan or loose-fitting coat.

Panel of 15 sts.

Row 1 (RS) Purl.

Row 2 Knit.

Row 3 P7, Make Bobble (MB) as follows: (k1, yo, k1, yo, k1) in next st, turn and p5, turn and k5, turn and p2 tog, p1, p2 tog; turn and sl 1, k2 tog, psso, completing bobble; p7.

Row 4 K7, p1-b, k7.

Row 5 P4, MB, p2, k1-b, p2, MB, p4.

Row 6 K4, p1-b, k2, p1, k2, p1-b, k4.

Row 7 P2, MB, p1, sl next st to cn and hold in front, p1, then k1 from cn (Front Cross, FC); p1, k1-b, p1, sl next st to cn and hold at back, k1, then p1 from cn (Back Cross, BC); p1, MB, p2.

Row 8 K2, p1-b, k2, (p1, k1) 3 times, k1, p1-b, k2.

Row 9 P2, FC, p1, FC, k1-b, BC, p1, BC, p2.

Row 10 K3, BC, k1, p3, k1, FC, k3.

Row 11 P4, FC, Make One (M1) p-wise by purling into the back of running thread; sl 1, k2 tog, psso, M1 p-wise, BC, p4.

Row 12 K5, BC, p1, FC, k5.

Row 13 P5, purl into front and back of next st, sl 1, k2 tog, psso, purl into front and back of next st, p5.

Row 14 K7, p1-b, k7.

Rows 15 and 16 Repeat rows 1 and 2.

Repeat rows 1 to 16.

EYELET & LACE

Decorative increases and decreases are worked beside each other on the same row to form eyelet and lace patterns (see pp10, 11). For delicate fabrics, it is usual to knit fine yarn on small needles but bear in mind that larger needles will produce a lacier fabric. Many interesting patterns include simple geometric repeats, progressing to elaborate fan shapes and butterfly designs.

Drop loop mesh

Materials Fine angora, lightweight wool, silk or cotton for fine summer days.

Uses Smock inset panel, or allover pattern for party dress or baby's shawl.

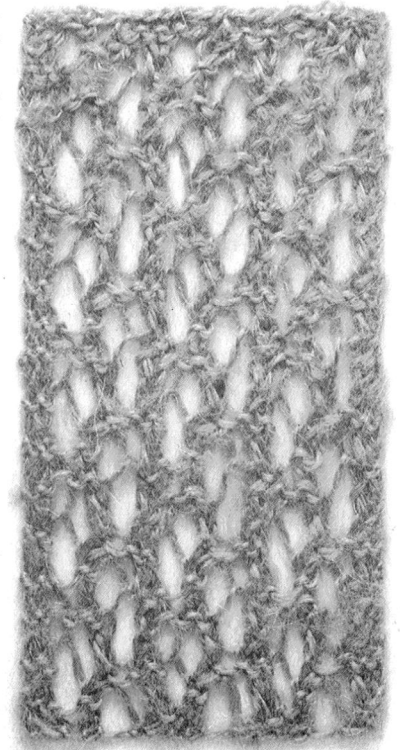

Multiple of 5 sts plus 3.

Note *Drop Loop (DL) : drop the second loop of the double yo of previous row off the needle. The first loop is already knitted.*

Preparation Row K3, *(yo) twice, k2 tog, k3; rep from *.

Row 1 K5, *DL, (yo) twice, k2 tog, k3; rep from *, end last repeat k1.

Row 2 K3, *DL, k2, (yo) twice, k2 tog, k1; rep from *.

Row 3 K3, *DL, (yo) twice, k2 tog, k3; rep from *.

Repeat rows 1 to 3.

Butterfly

Materials Light-weight wool, rayon, silk or synthetic yarn for a very special occasion.

Uses Skirt and jacket inset panel or child's party dress.

Multiple of 22 sts plus 1.

Note *Cluster – sl the given number of sts wyib, pass yarn to front, sl the same number of sts back to left needle, pass yarn to back, sl the same sts again wyib.*

Row 1 (RS) K1, *yo, (k1-b, p3) 5 times, k1-b, yo, k1; rep from *.

Row 2 P3, *(k3, p1) 4 times, k3, p5; rep from *, end last repeat p3.

Row 3 K1, *yo, k1-b, yo, (k1-b, p3) 5 times, (k1-b, yo) twice, k1; rep from *.

Row 4 P5, *(k3, p1) 4 times, k3, p9; rep from *, end last repeat p5.

Row 5 K1, *yo, k1-b, yo, sl 1, k1, psso, yo (k1-b, p2 tog, p1) 5 times, k1-b, yo, k2 tog, yo, k1-b, yo, k1; rep from *.

Row 6 P7, *(k2, p1) 4 times, k2, p13; rep from *, end last repeat p7.

Row 7 K1, *k1-b, (yo, sl 1, k1, psso) twice, yo, (k1-b, p2) 5 times, k1-b, yo, (k2 tog, yo) twice, k1-b, k1; repeat from *.

Row 8 P8, *(k2, p1) 4 times, k2, p15; rep from *, end last repeat p8.

Row 9 K2, *(yo, k2 tog) twice, yo, k1-b, yo, (k1-b, p2 tog) 5 times, (k1-b, yo) twice, (sl 1, k1, psso, yo) twice, k3; rep from *, end last repeat k2.

Rows 10 and 12 P10, *(k1, p1) 4 times, k1, p19; rep from *, end last repeat p10.

Row 11 Sl 1, k1, psso, *(yo, k2 tog) 3 times, k1-b, yo, (k1-b, p1) 5 times, k1-b, yo, k1-b, (sl 1, k1, psso, yo) 3 times, sl 2, k1, p2sso; rep from *, end last repeat k2 tog instead of sl 2, k1, p2sso.

Row 13 K1, *(k2 tog, yo) twice, k2 tog, k1, k1-b, yo, (sl 1, k1, psso) twice, sl 1, k2 tog, psso, (k2 tog) twice, yo, k1-b, k1, sl 1, k1, psso, (yo, sl 1, k1, psso) twice, k1; rep from *.

Row 14 Cluster 2, *p7, Cluster 5, p7, Cluster 3; rep from *, end last repeat Cluster 2 instead of Cluster 3.

Repeat rows 1 to 14.

Shooting star

Materials 3-ply or fine Shetland wool, silk or rayon for a special party look.

Uses Skirt inset panel for mother and daughter or all-over pattern for matching party top, jacket or evening scarf.

Multiple of 34 sts plus 2.

Row 1 (RS) K1, *k3, k2 tog, k4, yo, p2, (k2, yo, sl 1, k1, psso) 3 times, p2, yo, k4, sl 1, k1, psso, k3; rep from *, end k1.

Row 2 K1, *p2, p2 tog-b, p4, yo, p1, k2, (p2, yo, p2 tog) 3 times, k2, p1, yo, p4, p2 tog, p2; rep from *, end k1.

Row 3 K1, *k1, k2 tog, k4, yo, k2, p2, (k2, yo, sl 1, k1, psso) 3 times, p2, k2, yo, k4, sl 1, k1, psso, k1; rep from *, end k1.

Row 4 K1, *p2 tog-b, p4, yo, p3, k2, (p2, yo, p2 tog) 3 times, k2, p3, yo, p4, p2 tog; rep from *, end k1.

Rows 5 to 12 Repeat rows 1 to 4 twice more.

Row 13 K1, *yo, sl 1, k1, psso, k2, yo, sl 1, k1, psso, p2, yo, k4, sl 1, k1, psso, k6, k2 tog, k4, yo, p2, k2, yo, sl 1, k1, psso, k2; rep from *, end k1.

Row 14 K1, *yo, p2 tog, p2, yo, p2 tog, k2, p1, yo, p4, p2 tog, p4, p2 tog-b, p4, yo, p1, k2, p2, yo, p2 tog, p2; rep from *, end k1.

Row 15 K1, *yo, sl 1, k1, psso, k2, yo, sl 1, k1, psso, p2, k2, yo, k4, sl 1, k1, psso, k2, k2 tog, k4, yo, k2, p2, k2, yo, sl 1, k1, psso, k2; rep from *, end k1.

Row 16 K1, *yo, p2 tog, p2, yo, p2 tog, k2, p3, yo, p4, p2 tog, p2 tog-b, p4, yo, p3, k2, p2, yo, p2 tog, p2; rep from *, end k1.

Rows 17 to 24 Repeat rows 13 to 16 twice more.

Repeat rows 1 to 24.

Lace cable

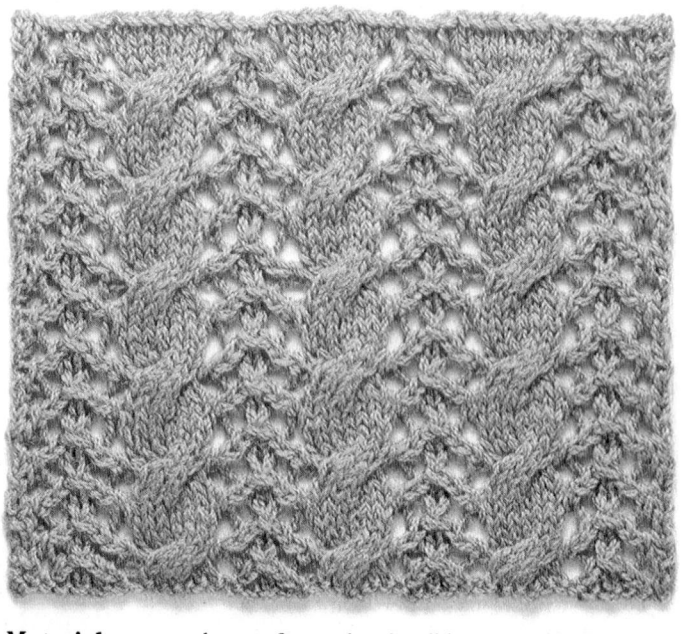

Materials 2- or 3-ply yarn for weekend walking; light-weight cotton or acrylic yarn for holiday wear.

Uses All-over design for short sleeved sweater, knee socks or stockings; overblouse or cardigan inset panel.

Multiple of 11 sts plus 7.

Row 1 *(WS) and all other WS rows* Purl.

Row 2 K1, *yo, sl 1, k1, psso, k1, k2 tog, yo, k6; rep from * to last 6 sts, end yo, sl 1, k1, psso, k1, k2 tog, yo, k1.

Row 4 K2, *yo, sl 1, k2 tog, psso, yo, k1, sl next 3 sts to cn and hold at back, k3, then k3 from cn, k1; rep from * to last 5 sts, end yo, sl 1, k2 tog, psso, yo, k2.

Row 6 Repeat row 2.

Row 8 K2, *yo, sl 1, k2 tog, psso, yo, k8; rep from * to last 5 sts, end yo, sl 1, k2 tog, psso, yo, k2.

Repeat rows 1 to 8.

Crazy check

Materials Fine wool, light-weight rayon or cotton yarn for summer sportswear.

Uses All-over design for T-shirts, sweaters for the family or man's tie.

Multiple of 16 sts plus 2.

Rows 1, 3, 5 and 7 (RS) k1,(sl 1, k1, psso, yo) 4 times, k8; rep from *, end k1.

Rows 2, 4, 6 and 8 K1, *k8, p8, rep from *, end k1.

Rows 9, 11, 13 and 15 K1, *k8, (yo, k2 tog) 4 times; rep from *, end k1.

Rows 10, 12, 14 and 16 K1, *p8, k8; rep from *, end k1.
Repeat rows 1 to 16.

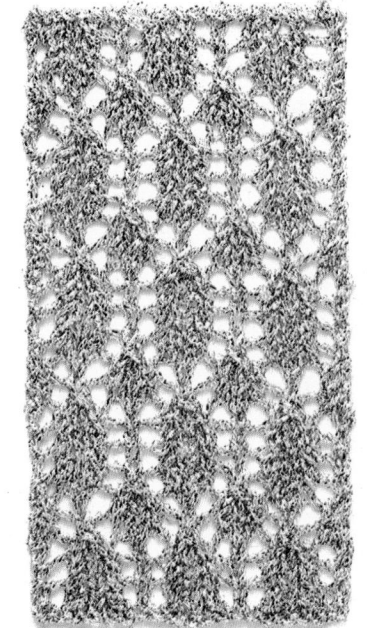

Beginner's lace

Materials 3-ply yarn or lurex for a classic style; cotton or synthetic for wash and wear.

Uses Shawl, sweater or cardigan inset panel; all-over repeat for placemat, traycloth or light throwover bedspread.

Multiple of 6 sts plus 1.

Row 1 *(WS) and all other WS rows* Purl.

Rows 2, 4 and 6 K1, *yo, sl 1, k1, psso, k1, k2 tog, yo, k1; rep from *.

Row 8 K2, *yo, sl 1, k2 tog, psso, yo, k3; rep from *, end last repeat k2.

Row 10 K1, *k2 tog, yo, k1, yo, sl 1, k1, psso, k1; rep from *.

Row 12 K2 tog, *yo, k3, yo, sl 1, k2 tog, psso; rep from *, end yo, k3, yo, sl 1, k1, psso.
Repeat rows 1 to 12.

Chinese lantern

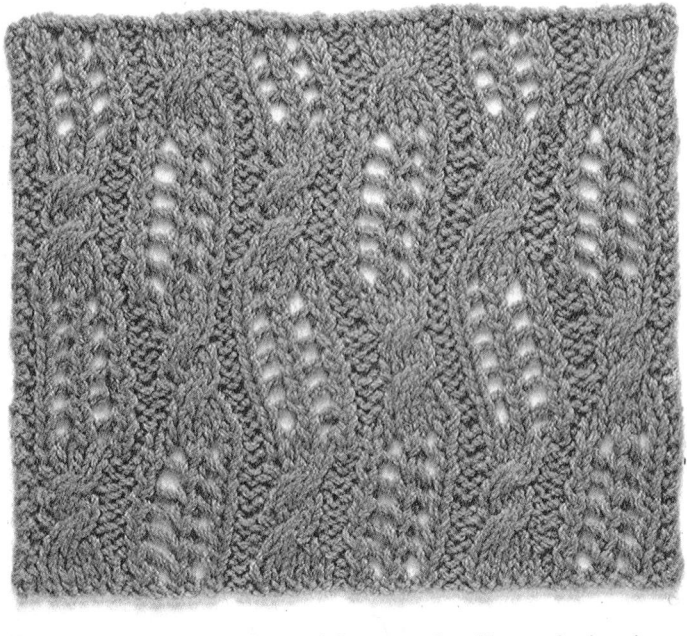

Materials Middle-weight wool for warmth; silk, synthetic mix or glitter yarn for evenings out.
Uses Bed jacket all-over design; inset panel for evening top or cape.

Multiple of 13 sts plus 2.

Row 1 (WS) K2, *p5, k1, p5, k2; rep from *.
Row 2 P2, *k1, (yo, k2 tog) twice, p1, k5, p2; rep from *.
Rows 3 and 5 K2, *p4, k2, p5, k2; rep from *.
Row 4 P2, *k1, (yo, k2 tog) twice, p2, k4, p2; rep from *.
Row 6 P2, *k1, (yo, k2 tog) twice, p2, sl next 2 sts to cn and hold at back, k2, then k2 from cn, p2; rep from *.
Rows 7, 8, 9, 10, 11 and 12 Repeat rows 3, 4, 5 and 6, then repeat rows 3 and 4 again.
Row 13 Repeat row 1.

Row 14 P2, *k5, p1, (sl 1, k1, psso, yo) twice, k1, p2; rep from *.
Rows 15 and 17 K2, *p5, k2, p4, k2; rep from *.
Row 16 P2, *k4, p2, (sl 1, k1, psso, yo) twice, k1, p2; rep from *.
Row 18 P2, *sl next 2 sts to cn and hold at back, k2, then k2 from cn; p2, (sl 1, k1, psso, yo) twice, k1, p2; rep from *.
Rows 19, 20, 21, 22, 23 and 24 Repeat rows 15, 16, 17 and 18, then rows 15 and 16 again.
Repeat rows 1 to 24.

Vienna lace

Materials Fine wool or rayon for a classic look; cotton or synthetic yarn for strength and washability.

Uses Sweater yoke or inset panel; all-over pattern for curtain, bed cover or pillow cover.

Multiple of 20 sts plus 2.

Row 1 *(WS) and all other WS rows* Purl, always working (k1, p1) into each double yo of a previous row.

Row 2 K1, yo, *sl 1, k1, psso, k2, yo, sl 1, k1, psso, k1, yo, k2 tog, p2, sl 1, k1, psso, yo, k1, k2 tog, yo, k2, k2 tog, (yo) twice; rep from *, end last repeat yo, k1 instead of (yo) twice.

Row 4 P2, *(yo, sl 1, k1, psso, k2) twice, p2, (k2, k2 tog, yo) twice, p2; rep from *.

Row 6 P2, *k1, yo, sl 1, k1, psso, k2, yo, sl 1, k1, psso, k1, p2, k1, k2 tog, yo, k2, k2 tog, k1, p2; rep from *.

Row 8 P2, *sl 1, k1, psso, (yo) twice, sl 1, k1, psso, k2, yo, sl 1, k1, psso, p2, k2 tog, yo, k2, k2 tog, (yo) twice, k2 tog, p2; rep from *.

Row 10 P2, *sl 1, k1, psso (yo) twice, k2 tog, k3, yo, sl 1, k1, psso, k2 tog, yo, k3, sl 1, k1, psso, (yo) twice, k2 tog, p2; rep from *.

Row 12 P2, *sl 1, k1, psso, (yo) twice, k2 tog, k1, k2 tog, yo, k4, yo, sl 1, k1, psso, k1, sl 1, k1, psso, (yo) twice, k2 tog, p2; rep from *.

Row 14 P2, *sl 1, k1, psso, (yo) twice, (k2 tog) twice, yo, k6, yo, (sl 1, k1, psso) twice, (yo) twice, k2 tog, p2; rep from *.

Row 16 P2, *sl 1, k1, psso, yo, k1, k2 tog, yo, k2, k2 tog, (yo) twice, sl 1, k1, psso, k2, yo, sl 1, k1, psso, k1, yo, k2 tog, p2; rep from *.

Row 18 P2, *(k2, k2 tog, yo) twice, p2, (yo, sl 1, k1, psso, k2), twice, p2; rep from *.

Row 20 P2, *k1, k2 tog, yo, k2, k2 tog, yo, k1, p2, k1, yo, sl 1, k1, psso, k2, yo, sl 1, k1, psso, k1, p2; rep from *.

Row 22 P2, *k2 tog, yo, k2, k2 tog, (yo) twice, k2 tog, p2, sl 1, k1, psso, (yo) twice, sl 1, k1, psso, k2, yo, sl 1, k1, psso, p2; rep from *.

Row 24 K1, *k2 tog, yo, k3, sl 1, k1, psso, (yo) twice, k2 tog, p2, sl 1, k1, psso, (yo) twice, k2 tog, k3, yo, sl 1, k1, psso; rep from *, end k1.

Row 26 K3, *yo, sl 1, k1, psso, k1, sl 1, k1, psso, (yo) twice) k2 tog, p2, sl 1, k1, psso, (yo) twice, k2 tog, k1, k2 tog, yo, k4; rep from *, end last repeat k3.

Row 28 K4, *yo, (sl 1, k1, psso) twice, (yo) twice, k2 tog, p2, sl 1, k1, psso, (yo) twice, (k2 tog) twice, yo, k6; rep from *, end last repeat k4.

Repeat rows 1 to 28.

Ricrac

Materials 3-ply crêpe wool or cotton yarn for a summery look; metallic or rayon for evening elegance.

Uses All-over design for collared sweater or sleeveless overblouse; loose-fitting jacket or shawl.

Multiple of 10 sts plus 5.

Row 1 (RS) K1, *sl 1, k1, psso, yo, k5, k2 tog, yo, k1; rep from *, end sl 1, k1, psso, yo, k2.

Row 2 P1, *p2 tog, yo, p2, yo, p1, p2 tog, p3; rep from *, end p2 tog, yo, p2.

Row 3 K1, *sl 1, k1, psso, yo, k3, k2 tog, k2, yo, k1; rep from *, end sl 1, k1, psso, yo, k2.

Row 4 P1, *p2 tog, yo, p2, yo, p3, p2 tog, p1; rep from *, end p2 tog, yo, p2.

Row 5 K1, *sl 1, k1, psso, yo, k2, sl 1, k1, psso, k3, yo, k1; rep from *, end sl 1, k1, psso, yo, k2.

Row 6 P1, *p2 tog, yo, p2, yo, p3, p2 tog-b, p1; rep from *, end p2 tog, yo, p2.

Row 7 K1, *sl 1, k1, psso, yo, k2, yo, sl 1, k1, psso, k4; rep from *, end sl 1, k1, psso, yo, k2.

Row 8 P1, *p2 tog, yo, p4, p2 tog-b, p1, yo, p1; rep from *, end p2 tog, yo, p2.

Row 9 K1, *sl 1, k1, psso, (yo, k2) twice, sl 1, k1, psso, k2; rep from *, end sl 1, k1, psso, yo, k2.

Row 10 P1, *p2 tog, yo, p2 tog-b, p3, yo, p1; rep from *, end p2 tog, yo, p2.

Row 11 K1, *sl 1, k1, psso, yo, k2, yo, k3, k2 tog, k1; rep from *, end sl 1, k1, psso, yo, k2.

Row 12 P1, *p2 tog, yo, p2, p2 tog, p3, yo, p1; rep from *, end p2 tog, yo, p2.

Repeat rows 1 to 12.

EDGINGS & BORDERS

*Edging and border patterns are mostly decorative
and lacy. They are designed as a trim for plain edges
of knitted or woven fabric garments or many household
items. Edges can be knitted in yarns such as lurex, silk
or string and can be sewn on or incorporated into knitting
as a fancy border. Patterns include curves,
points, partridge shapes and picots (see pp10, 11).*

Leaf edging

Materials 2-ply wool, silk or rayon yarn for a contrast trim.
Uses Wool dress bodice, collar and cuffs, skirt hem, cardigan or
loose-fitting waistcoat.

Cast on 8sts.
Row 1 (RS) K5, yo, k1, yo, k2.
Row 2 P6, knit into front and
back of next st (inc), k3.
Row 3 K4, p1, k2, yo, k1, yo, k3.
Row 4 P8, inc in next st, k4.
Row 5 K4, p2, k3, yo, k1, yo, k4.
Row 6 P10, inc in next st, k5.
Row 7 K4, p3, k4, yo, k1, yo, k5.
Row 8 P12, inc in next st, k6.
Row 9 K4, p4, sl 1, k1, psso, k7,
k2 tog, k1.
Row 10 P10, inc in next st, k7.
Row 11 K4, p5, sl 1, k1, psso,
k5, k2 tog, k1.
Row 12 P8, inc in next st, k2,
p1, k5.
Row 13 K4, p1, k1, p4, sl 1, k1,
psso, k3, k2 tog, k1.
Row 14 P6, inc in next st, k3,
p1, k5.
Row 15 K4, p1, k1, p5, sl 1, k1,
psso, k1, k2 tog, k1.
Row 16 P4, inc in next st, k4,
p1, k5.
Row 17 K4, p1, k1, p6, sl 1, k2
tog, psso, k1.
Row 18 P2 tog, cast off next 5
sts using p2 tog st to cast off
first st; p3, k4.
Repeat rows 1 to 18.

Faggot and scallop

Materials Light-weight yarn or crochet cotton for household trim.
Uses Edging for bedlinen, pillows or traycloth.

Cast on 13 sts.

Row 1 *(WS) and all other WS rows* K2, purl to last 2 sts, k2.
Row 2 K7, yo, sl 1, k1, psso, yo, k4.
Row 4 K6, (yo, sl 1, k1, psso) twice, yo, k4.
Row 6 K5, (yo, sl 1, k1, psso) 3 times, yo, k4.
Row 8 K4, (yo, sl 1, k1, psso) 4 times, yo, k4.
Row 10 K3, (yo, sl 1, k1, psso), 5 times, yo, k4.

Row 12 K4, (yo, sl 1, k1, psso) 5 times, k2 tog, k2.
Row 14 K5, (yo, sl 1, k1, psso) 4 times, k2 tog, k2.
Row 16 K6, (yo, sl 1, k1, psso) 3 times, k2 tog, k2.
Row 18 K7, (yo, sl 1, k1, psso) twice, k2 tog, k2.
Row 20 K8, yo, sl 1, k1, psso, k2 tog, k2.
Repeat rows 1 to 20.

Seashore edging

Materials Fine cotton for a dainty look; lurex for added luxury.
Uses Print cushion trim; towel or bathroom set finish.

Cast on 13 sts.

Row 1 *and all other odd-numbered rows.* K2, purl to last 2 sts, k2. (Number of purl sts will vary on different rows.)
Row 2 Sl 1, k3, yo, k5, yo, k2 tog, yo, k2.
Row 4 Sl 1, k4, sl 1, k2 tog, psso, k2, (yo, k2 tog) twice, k1.
Row 6 Sl 1, k3, sl 1, k1, psso,

k2, (yo, k2 tog) twice, k1.
Row 8 Sl 1, k2, sl 1, k1, psso, k2, (yo, k2 tog) twice, k1.
Row 10 Sl 1, k1, sl 1, k1, psso, k2, (yo, k2 tog) twice, k1.
Row 12 K1, sl 1, k1, psso, k2, yo, k1, yo, k2 tog, yo, k2.
Row 14 Sl 1, (k3, yo) twice, k2 tog, yo, k2.
Repeat rows 1 to 14.

Peak edging

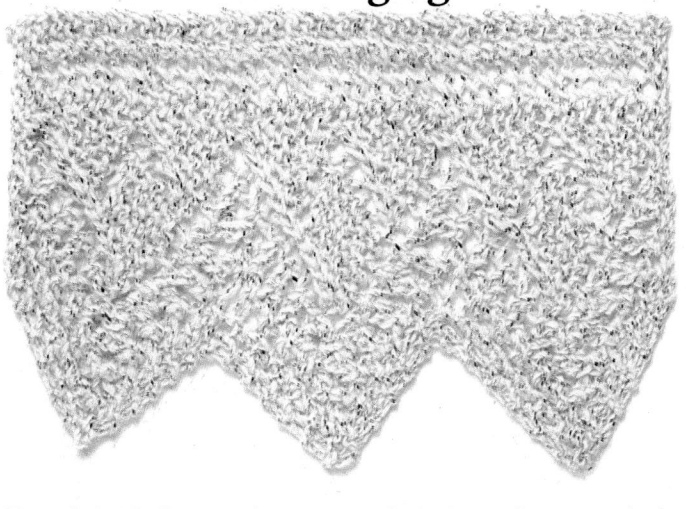

Materials Medium crochet cotton or flecked yarn for a pretty look.
Uses Trim for triangular print shawl, lower edge of fabric overblouse,
bed linen, buffet runner or tablecloth.

Cast on 17 sts and knit one row.

Section A of pattern: K2, k1-b,
yo, k1, p2 tog, (yo) twice, (p2
tog) twice, yo. (10 sts inc to 11).
Section B of pattern: K2, p2 tog,
yo, (p2 tog) twice, (yo) twice, p2
tog, yo, p2 tog. (12 sts dec to 11).
Row 1 (RS) K4, yo, p2 tog, k2,
yo, k2, p1, k3, yo, k1-b, k2.
Row 2 A, k5, yo, p2 tog, k2.
Row 3 (K4, yo, p2 tog) twice,
k1, p1, k3, yo, k1-b, k2.
Row 4 A, k7, yo, p2 tog, k2.
Row 5 K4, yo, p2 tog, k6, yo,
p2 tog, k1, p1, k3, yo, k1-b, k2.
Row 6 A, k9, yo, p2 tog, k2.
Row 7 K4, yo, p2 tog, k5, k2
tog, yo, k1, yo, p2 tog, k1, p1,
k3, yo, k1-b, k2.
Row 8 A, k3, yo, p2 tog, k6, yo,
p2 tog, k2.
Row 9 K4, yo, p2 tog, k3, k2
tog, yo, k5, yo, p2 tog, k1, p1,
k3, yo, k1-b, k2.
Row 10 A, k7, yo, p2 tog, k4,
yo, p2 tog, k2.
Row 11 K4, yo, p2 tog, k1, k2
tog, yo, k9, yo, k3, p1, k3, yo,
k1-b, k2.
Row 12 K2, k1-b, yo, k1, p2
tog, (yo) twice, p2 tog, p3 tog,

yo, k11, (yo, p2 tog, k2) twice.
Row 13 K4, yo, p2 tog, k2, yo,
sl 1, k1, psso, k7, k2 tog, yo, k4,
p1, p2 tog, yo, p2 tog, k2.
Row 14 K2, p2 tog, yo, (p2 tog)
twice, (yo) twice, p2 tog, k1, yo,
p2 tog, k5, p2 tog-b, yo, k5, yo,
p2 tog, k2.
Row 15 K4, yo, p2 tog, k4, yo,
sl 1, k1, psso, k3, k2 tog, yo, k1,
p2 tog, k1, p1, p2 tog, yo, p2
tog, k2.
Row 16 B, k1, p2 tog-b, yo, k7,
yo, p2 tog, k2.
Row 17 K4, yo, p2 tog, k6, yo,
k3 tog, yo, k3, p1, p2 tog, yo,
p2 tog, k2.
Row 18 B, k8, yo, p2 tog, k2.
Row 19 K4, yo, p2 tog, k5, k2
tog, yo, k3, p1, p2 tog, yo, p2
tog, k2.
Row 20 B, k6, yo, p2 tog, k2.
Row 21 K4, yo, p2 tog, k3, k2
tog, yo, k3, p1, p2 tog, yo, p2
tog, k2.
Row 22 B, k4, yo, p2 tog, k2.
Row 23 K4, yo, p2 tog, k1, k2
tog, yo, k3, p1, p2 tog, yo, p2 tog, k2.
Row 24 B, k2, yo, p2 tog, k2.
Repeat rows 1 to 24.

Christmas tree

Materials Angora for warmth; random-dyed rayon or fine crochet cotton for special table linen.
Uses Shawl or blanket border; placemat, buffet runner or tablecloth.

Cast on 16 sts and knit one row.

Row 1 Yo, k2 tog, k1, yo, k10, yo, k2 tog, k1.
Row 2 K2, yo, k2 tog, k12, p1.
Row 3 Yo, k2 tog, k1, yo, k2 tog, yo, k9, yo, k2 tog, k1.
Row 4 K2, yo, k2 tog, k13, p1.
Row 5 Yo, k2 tog, k1, (yo, k2 tog) twice, yo, k8, yo, k2 tog, k1.
Row 6 K2, yo, k2 tog, k14, p1.
Row 7 Yo, k2 tog, k1, (yo, k2 tog) 3 times, yo, k7, yo, k2 tog, k1.
Row 8 K2, yo, k2 tog, k15, p1.
Row 9 Yo, k2 tog, k1, (yo, k2 tog) 4 times, yo, k6, yo, k2 tog, k1.
Row 10 K2, yo, k2 tog, k16, p1.
Row 11 Yo, k2 tog, k1, (yo, k2 tog), 5 times, yo, k5, yo, k2 tog, k1.
Row 12 K2, yo, k2 tog, k17, p1.
Row 13 Yo, k2 tog, k1, (yo, k2 tog) 6 times, yo, k4, yo, k2 tog, k1.
Row 14 K2, yo, k2, tog, k18, p1.
Row 15 Yo, k2 tog, k1, (yo, k2 tog) 7 times, yo, k3, yo, k2 tog, k1.
Row 16 K2, yo, k2 tog, k19, p1.
Row 17 Yo, (k2 tog) twice, (yo, k2 tog) 7 times, k3, yo, k2 tog, k1.
Rows 18, 20, 22, 24, 26, 28, 30 Repeat rows 14, 12, 10, 8, 6, 4 and 2.
Row 19 Yo, (k2 tog) twice, (yo, k2 tog) 6 times, k4, yo, k2 tog, k1.
Row 21 Yo, (k2 tog) twice, (yo, k2 tog) 5 times, k5, yo, k2 tog, k1.
Row 23 Yo, (k2 tog) twice, (yo, k2 tog) 4 times, k6, yo, k2 tog, k1.
Row 25 Yo, (k2 tog) twice, (yo, k2 tog) 3 times, k7, yo, k2 tog, k1.
Row 27 Yo, (k2 tog) twice, (yo, k2 tog) twice, k8, yo, k2 tog, k1.
Row 29 Yo, (k2 tog) twice, yo, k2 tog, k9, yo, k2 tog, k1.
Row 31 Yo, (k2 tog) twice, k10, yo, k2 tog, k1.
Row 32 K2, yo, k2 tog, k11, p1.
Repeat rows 1 to 32.

Ripple and cube

Materials 2-ply wool, rayon, flecked synthetic, fine cotton, lurex or silk for a lacy finish.
Uses Mother and daughter shawl trim or matching collar and cuffs.

Cast on 17 sts and knit one row.

Row 1 (RS) K4, (yo, k1, k2 tog) twice, yo, k3, yo, k4.
Row 2 K4, yo, k5, (yo, p2 tog, k1) twice, yo, k4.
Row 3 K4, (yo, k1, k2 tog) twice, yo, k1, yo, sl 1, k1, psso, k1, k2 tog, yo, k1, yo, k4.
Row 4 K4, yo, k3, yo, p3 tog, yo, k3, (yo, p2 tog, k1) twice, yo, k4.
Row 5 K5, k2 tog, yo, k1, k2 tog, yo, k11, yo, k4.
Row 6 K2 tog, k3, yo, p2 tog, k1, p2 tog-b, yo, k1, yo, p2 tog, k1, p2 tog-b, (yo, k1, p2 tog) twice, k4.
Row 7 K4, (yo, sl 1, k1, psso, k1) twice, yo, sl 1, k2 tog, psso, yo, k3, yo, k3 tog, yo, k3, k2 tog.
Row 8 K2 tog, k3, yo, p2 tog, k3, p2 tog-b, (yo, k1, p2 tog-b) twice, yo, k2 tog, k3.
Row 9 K3, k2 tog, yo, sl 1, k1, psso, (k1, yo, sl 1, k1, psso) twice, k1, k2 tog, yo, k3, k2 tog.
Row 10 K2 tog, k3, yo, p3 tog, (yo, k1, p2 tog-b) twice, yo, k2 tog, k3.
Row 11 K3, k2 tog, yo, sl 1, k1, psso, k1, yo, sl 1, k1, psso, k2, yo, k3, k2 tog.
Row 12 K2 tog, k3, yo, k1, (yo, p2 tog, k1) twice, yo, k4.
Repeat rows 1 to 12.

Partridge edging

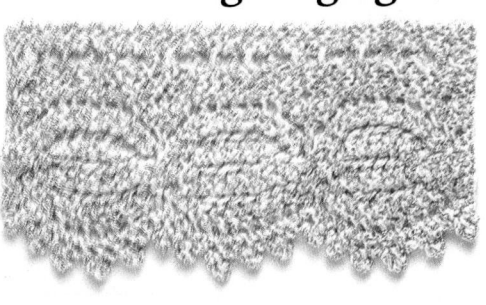

Materials 2-ply wool or random-dyed silk for a special occasion.
Uses Baby shawl or evening wrap.

Cast on 18 sts and knit one row.

Notes *Cable needle required. DL :
drop the yo of previous row off
needle. Inc. In this pattern knit
into yo of previous row.*
*Cast on 2 and cast off 2 – Knit
first st, leaving it on needle, and
place new st on left needle ; then
knit this st and place next new st
on left needle. Then k2 (the 2 new
sts) and pass the first st over the
second ; then knit the third st (the
original first st) and pass the
second st over it. This completes
one picot point.*

Preparation Row K5, k2 tog,
k2, yo, k1, k2 tog, yo, k2 tog,
k1, yo, k3.

Row 1 Sl 1, k2, yo, slip the yo of
previous row, k2, inc, k3, sl next
2 sts to cn and hold in front, k3,
then k2 from cn, yo, k2 tog, k1.

Row 2 Cast on 2 and cast off 2,
k6, k2 tog, yo, k2 tog, k4, (k1,
p1) into both yo loops together,
as if they were a single loop, k3.

Row 3 Sl 1, k1, k2 tog, yo, k2
tog, k10, yo, k2 tog, k1.

Row 4 K5, (yo, k1) twice, k2
tog, yo, k2 tog, k3, yo, DL, k3.

Row 5 Sl 1, k2, (k1, p1) into the
yo of previous row, k7, inc, k1,
inc, k2, yo, k2 tog, k1.

Row 6 Cast on 2 and cast off 2,
k4, yo, k2, yo, k2 tog, k1, yo,
(k1, k2 tog, yo, k2 tog)
twice, k2.

Row 7 Sl 1, k2, yo, DL, k6, (yo,
k2 tog, k1) 4 times.

Row 8 K5, (yo, k2 tog, k1) 3

times, yo, k2 tog, k2, (k1, p1)
into the yo of previous row, k3.

Row 9 Sl 1, k1, k2 tog, yo, k2
tog, k5, (yo, k2 tog, k1) 4 times.

Row 10 Cast on 2 and cast off 2
k4, (yo, k2 tog, k1) 3 times, yo,
k2 tog, k2, yo, DL, k3.

Row 11 Sl 1, k2, (k1, p1) into the
yo of previous row, k6, (yo, k2
tog, k1) 4 times.

Row 12 K5, (yo, k2 tog, k1) 4
times, k2 tog, yo, k2 tog, k2.

Rows 13 and 15 Repeat rows 7
and 9.

Row 14 Cast on 2 and cast off 2,
k4, (yo, k2 tog, k1) 3 times, yo,
k2 tog, k2, (k1, p1) into the yo
of previous row, k3.

Row 16 K5, (yo, k2 tog, k1) 3
times, yo, k2 tog, k2, yo, DL, k3.

Row 17 Sl 1, k2, (k1, p1) into the
yo of previous row, k6, yo, (k2
tog, k1) twice, (yo, k2 tog, k1)
twice.

Row 18 Cast on 2 and cast off 2,
k4, yo, k2 tog, k1, k2 tog, yo, k2
tog, k1, yo, k3, k2 tog, yo, k2
tog, k2.

Row 19 Sl 1, k2, yo, DL, k7, yo,
k2 tog, k2, (yo, k2 tog, k1) twice.

Row 20 K5, yo, (k2 tog) twice,
yo, k2 tog, k1, yo, k5, (k1, p1)
into the yo of previous row, k3.

Row 21 Sl 1, k1, k2 tog, yo, k2
tog, k7, (k2 tog, k1) twice, yo,
k2 tog, k1.

Row 22 K5, k2 tog, k2, yo, k1,
k2 tog, yo, k2 tog, k1, yo, DL, k3.
Repeat rows 1 to 22.

Faggot and diamond

Materials 2- or 3-ply wool for a fine lacy look; random-dyed rayon or cotton yarn for furnishing.
Uses Baby's shawl or carriage set; bedspread or blind edging.

Cast on 34 sts and knit one row.

Row 1 Sl 1, k3, yo, sl 1, k1, psso, k3, k2 tog, yo, p3, yo, sl 1, k1, psso, k3, yo, sl 1, k1, psso, (yo, k2 tog) 6 times, k1.
Row 2 Sl 1, k23, p5, k3, (k1, p1) in next st, k1.
Row 3 Sl 1, k5, yo, sl 1, k1, psso, k1, k2 tog, yo, p5, yo, sl 1, k1, psso, k3, (yo, k2 tog) 6 times, k2.
Row 4 Sl 1, k24, p3, k5, (k1, p1) in next st, k1.
Row 5 Sl 1, k7, yo, sl 1, k2 tog, psso, yo, p7, yo, sl 1, k1, psso, k3, (yo, k2 tog) 6 times, k1.
Row 6 Sl 1, k25, p1, k7, (k1, p1) in next st, k1.
Row 7 Sl 1, k6, k2 tog, yo, k3,

yo, p2 tog, p3, p2 tog-b, yo, k3, k2 tog, yo, k1-b, (yo, k2 tog) 5 times, k2.
Row 8 Sl 1, k24, p3, k6, k2 tog, k1.
Row 9 Sl 1, k4, k2 tog, yo, k5. yo, p2 tog, p1, p2 tog-b, yo, k3, k2 tog, yo, k1-b, (yo, k2 tog) 6 times, k1.
Row 10 Sl 1, k23, p5, k4, k2 tog, k1.
Row 11 Sl 1, k2, k2 tog, yo, k7, yo, p3 tog, yo, k3, k2 tog, yo, k1-b, (yo, k2 tog) 6 times, k2.
Row 12 Sl 1, k21, p7, k2, k2 tog, k2.
Repeat rows 1 to 12.

Diamond eyelet

Materials Shetland 2-ply for a dainty look; fine cotton yarn for household trim.
Uses Shawl edging; table linen or special picture mount.

Cast on 17 sts.

Note *Yo2, a double yo. All single purl sts on even-numbered rows go into the* second *loop of a double yo made on a preceding row.*

Row 1 K3, (yo, p2 tog) twice, k10.

Row 2 K12, (yo, p2 tog) twice, k1.

Row 3 K3, (yo, p2 tog) twice, k6, k2 tog, yo2, k1, inc in last st.

Row 4 K4, p1, k9, (yo, p2 tog) twice, k1.

Row 5 K3, (yo, p2 tog) twice, k4, k2 tog, yo2, (k2 tog) twice, yo2, k1, inc in last st.

Row 6 K4, p1, k3, p1, k7, (yo, p2 tog) twice, k1.

Row 7 K3, (yo, p2 tog) twice, k2, k2 tog [yo2, (k2 tog) twice] twice, yo2, k1, inc in last st.

Row 8 K4, (p1, k3) twice, p1, k5, (yo, p2 tog) twice, k1.

Row 9 K3, (yo, p2 tog) twice, k2 tog, [yo2, (k2 tog) twice] 3 times, yo2, k2 tog.

Row 10 K2, (p1, k3) 4 times, (yo, p2 tog) twice, k1.

Row 11 K3, (yo, p2 tog) twice, k2, k2 tog, [yo2, (k2 tog) twice] 3 times.

Row 12 K2 tog, k1, (p1, k3) twice, p1, k5, (yo, p2 tog) twice, k1.

Row 13 K3, (yo, p2 tog) twice, k4, k2 tog, [yo 2, (k2 tog) twice] twice.

Row 14 K2 tog, k1, p1, k3, p1, k7, (yo, p2 tog) twice, k1.

Row 15 K3, (yo, p2 tog) twice, k6, k2 tog, yo2, (k2 tog) twice.

Row 16 K2 tog, k1, p1, k9, (yo, p2 tog) twice, k1.

Repeat rows 1 to 16.

COLORWORK

Colorwork patterns with more than two colors in a row are usually charted on graph paper, where one square represents one stitch. These charts should be read upward from the bottom right-hand corner. Begin with a knit row and continue throughout in stocking stitch. Three or four stitches may be stranded but for larger areas, use separate bobbins of yarn (see pp12, 13). Chart single motifs, borders or all-over geometric patterns.

Sheep

Materials 4-ply, random-dyed, bouclé or mohair for a fun effect.
Uses Single motif for cushion set, picture panel or baby's crib cover or border repeat for child's jacket, blanket or rug.

For a fluffy "sheep's wool" effect, choose either bouclé yarn or tease out knitting worsted wool. Work duplicate stitch birds and flowers, (see p90).

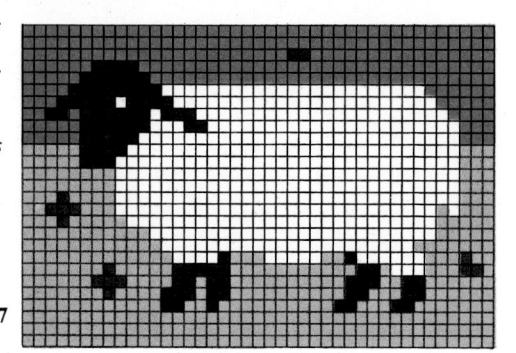

Repeat: 41 sts × 27 rows

Chevron

Materials Soft 4-ply wool or rayon for a figure-flattering, classic look.
Uses Dress bodice or sleeve band; all-over pattern for V-neck pullover or dress and matching loose jacket.

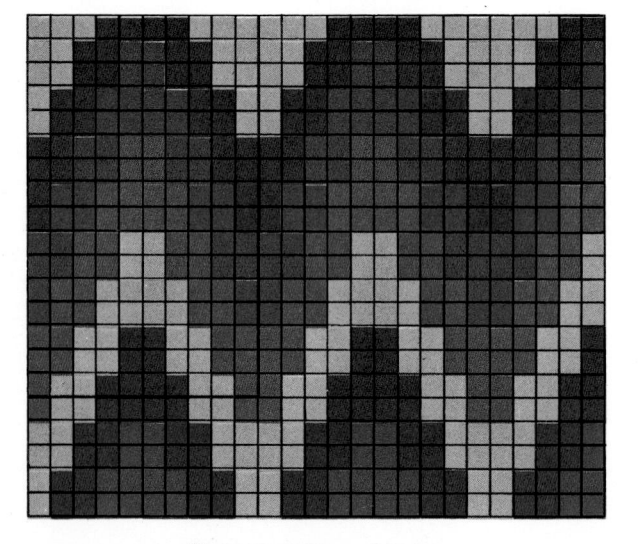

Repeat: 10 sts × 16 rows

Diagonals

Materials 4-ply wool for town wear; knitting worsted or thicker yarn for a warm woven plaid.

Uses Vest front panel, inset band for loose cardigan or crib cover; all-over pattern for lined jerkin or leg warmers.

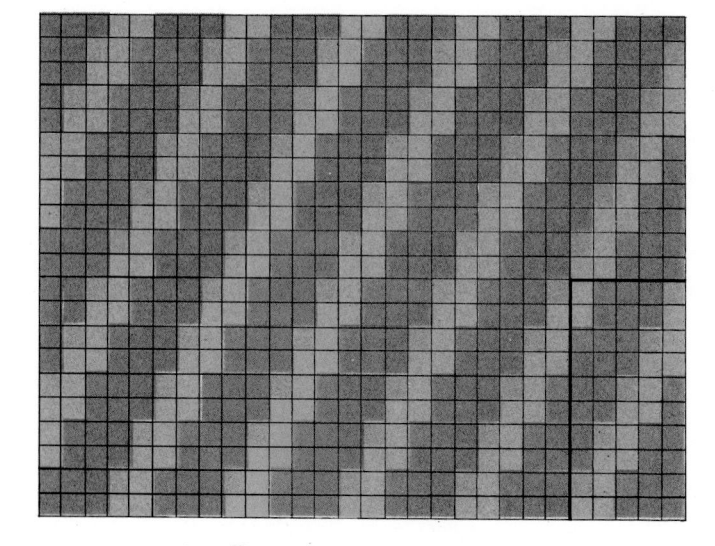

Repeat: 5 sts × 10 rows

Diabolo

Materials Knitting worsted wool, chenille, Shetland or acrylic yarn for sporty color combinations.
Uses Jacket or sweater inset band or all-over pattern for a simple slipover or cushion border.

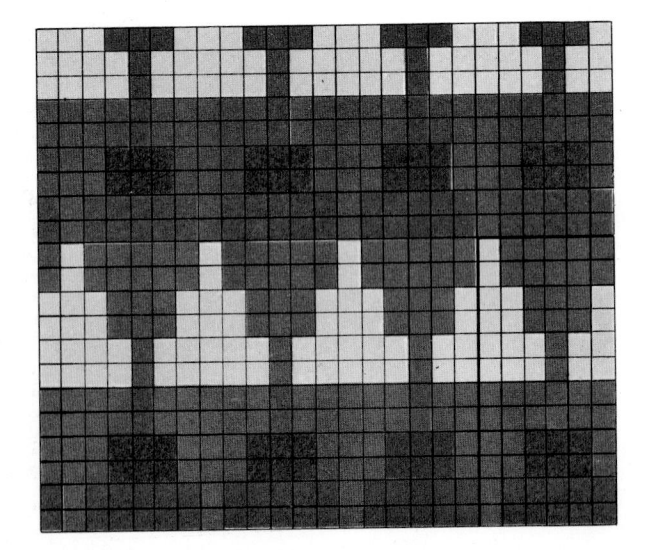

Repeat: 6 sts × 12 rows

Crescents

Materials Medium-weight crêpe yarn or acrylic for a sporty look.
Uses Sweater yoke or inset panel, waistcoat front or all-over repeat
for mittens, scarf or hat.

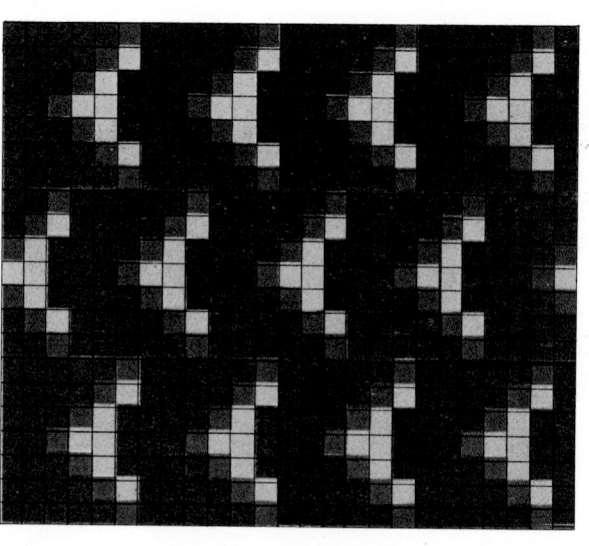

Repeat: 6 sts × 14 rows

Diamond and cross

Materials Shetland wool or medium-weight yarn for weekend wear; heavier wool for a winter sport look.

Uses Inset band for multi-patterned sweater or socks; chunky, hooded jacket inset band across chest and sleeve.

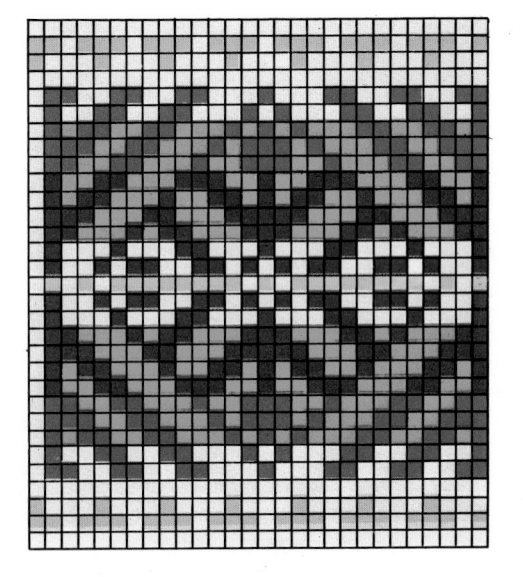

Repeat: 28 sts × 31 rows

Snowflake

Materials Fine Shetland yarn for spring wear; medium to heavy-weight wool for winter skiing.

Uses All-over repeat for classic slipover; ski sweater chest and sleeve inset bands with matching bobble hat and scarf.

Repeat: 32 sts × 33 rows

Tulips

Materials Chunky or knitting worsted for town and travel; 4-ply crêpe, silk or synthetic yarn for a pretty, classic look.

Uses Inset panel or border for knee-length coat, hooded cape, rug or poncho; all-over repeat for a slim-line suit or cushion set.

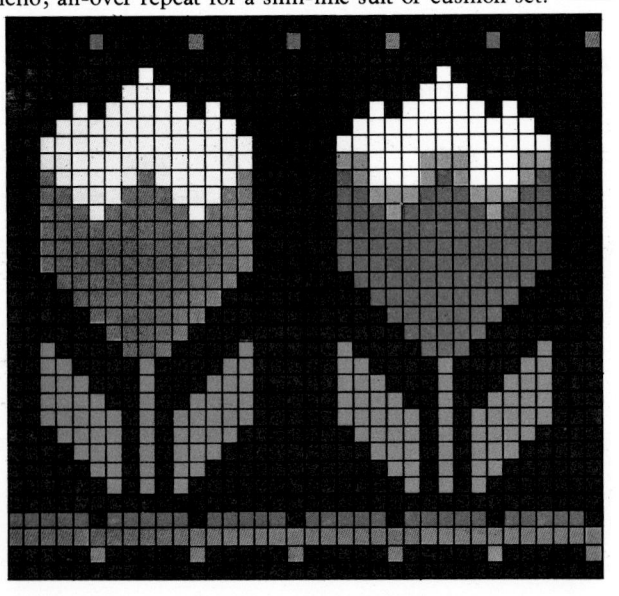

Repeat: 36 sts × 33 rows

84

Strawberry

Materials 4-ply wool, bouclé or rayon for a bright young look; chenille or chunky yarn for a bold effect.

Uses Motif for blouson back panel or all-over repeat for baggy-style sweater or cushion; inset band for jacket or blanket border.

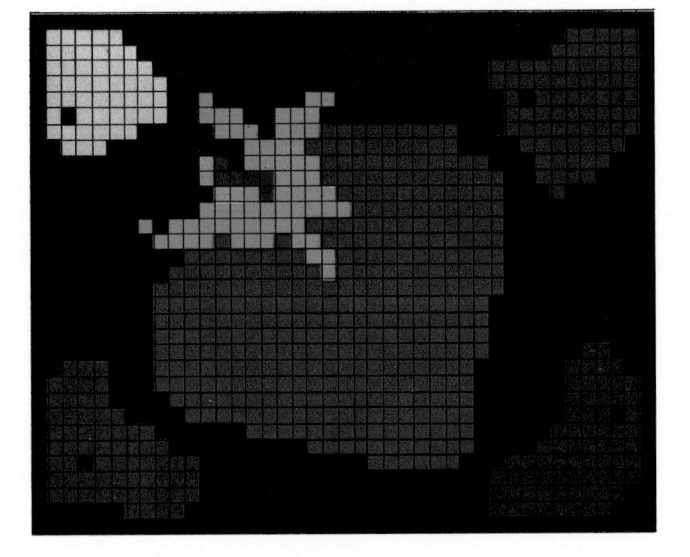

Repeat: 41 sts × 33 rows

Cross and stripe

Materials Fine wool or 3-ply synthetic mix for a spring look; chunky yarn for family ski wear.

Uses Sweater yoke or inset band or all-over pattern for scarf and bobble hats; inset panel for hooded cardigan, socks or mittens.

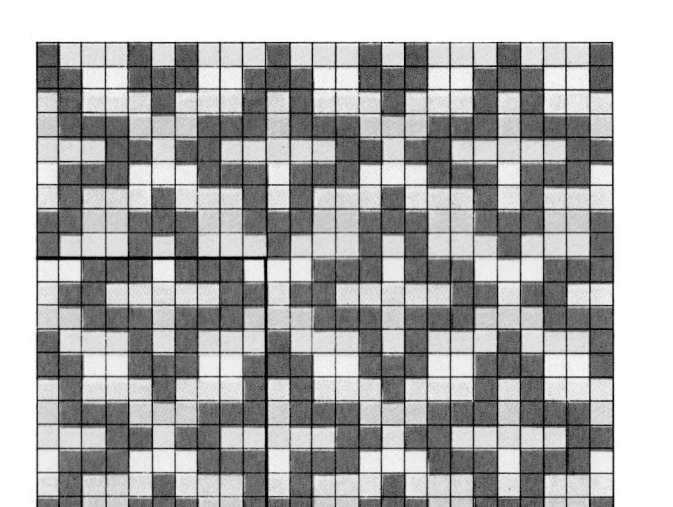

Repeat: 10 sts × 12 rows

Dots

Materials Knitting worsted wool with novelty mix or acrylic yarn for a rich tweedy effect.

Uses All-over pattern for vest front, slipover, toddler's coat and hat, matching mitts and scarf.

Repeat: 8 sts × 4 rows

Balloons

Materials Silk and lurex for a bright, showy effect; middle-weight yarn for a sporty look.

Uses Party dress top or inset panel for box-style bolero; all-over repeat for sweater or waistcoat front.

Repeat: 10 sts × 16 rows

EMBROIDERY

*With the exception of honeycombing (see p91)
these embroidery patterns may be applied as colorful
and spontaneous motifs to any knitted fabric. Appliqué
and freehand embroidery can be worked directly onto
the fabric but you may prefer to chart your cross
stitch or Duplicate stitch designs. Always use a large
blunt-ended yarn needle and, in general, keep
your embroidery relaxed so that the tension
is similar to that of the knitting.*

Cross stitching

Materials Wool, crêpe, rayon, silk or cotton (equal in thickness to background yarn) for a personalized look.
Uses Spot motif for child's sweater, hat, scarf or mitts.

Work a row of diagonal stitches from R to L first, and complete the crosses by working back along the row in the opposite direction.

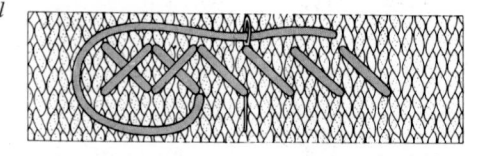

Cross stitch is best worked on a stocking stitch background. Each cross should be square, counted over, eg., two stitches and two rows, (blocked) or two stitches and three rows (unblocked). Insert needle vertically so that the elasticity of knitting does not pull embroidery out of shape.

Duplicate stitch

Materials Wool, cotton, silk or synthetic yarns (equal in weight to background fabric) for a nostalgic note.

Uses Single motif for sweater, cardigan or dress bodice and tied with a real ribbon bow.

1 *Secure yarn to WS. Bring needle through middle of 1st st. Re-insert under st above.*

2 *Draw needle through, insert under base of 1st and next st. Work 2nd row upside-down.*

Quick and easy duplicate stitching is best worked with a blunt-ended yarn needle on a close-knit fabric such as stockinette stitch where it gives the impression of having been knitted in. The embroidery forms a double fabric so, as well as for motifs, it is particularly useful for reinforcing elbows and other areas of garments that get a lot of wear.

Honeycombing

Materials Fine or medium-weight cotton, rayon or wool ribbed knitting for party wear. Self- or contrast-colored yarn (equal in weight to background fabric) for honeycombing.
Uses Dress or blouse yoke, inset panel, waistband or cuffs.

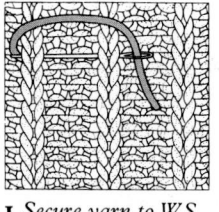

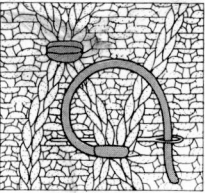

1 *Secure yarn to W S. Bring needle through to L of k st and insert it from R to L under k st of next rib and under 1st k st. Draw tight and repeat back stitch once.*

2 *Insert needle vertically to R of back sts and draw it through at L of k st 5 rows below.*

3 *Insert needle from R to L under k st of next rib and under 1st k st. Draw tight and repeat back stitch once more. Insert needle vertically and draw through at L of k st 5 rows above.*

Honeycombing is a form of smocking worked on ribbed knitting – p3, k1 makes an ideal background rib. Where you wish to use it to control fullness in a garment, remember to cast on enough stitches to give at least 1½ times the finished width. Before you begin to embroider, remember to check that you have the right multiple of stitches at that point.

Appliqué

Materials Fine cotton, acrylic or medium-weight wool for a real fun effect.

Uses Cardigan pocket, T-shirt or sweater motif. May be pinned or softly padded for a three-dimensional picture pattern.

Pin steam-pressed initials in place and hem, picking up one strand from background and one from edge of letter.

Knitting appliqué can be fun. These block-type initials are knitted in stocking stitch and shaped by simply increasing or casting off stitches, according to the shape of your letter. Use matching yarn to hem in place.

Bead and sequin

Materials Fine stranded cotton or silk, *coton à broder*, sequins and beads for added dazzle.

Uses Spot motif for dress or sweater shoulder or repeat pattern for cardigan front panel or knitted picture.

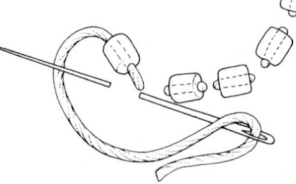

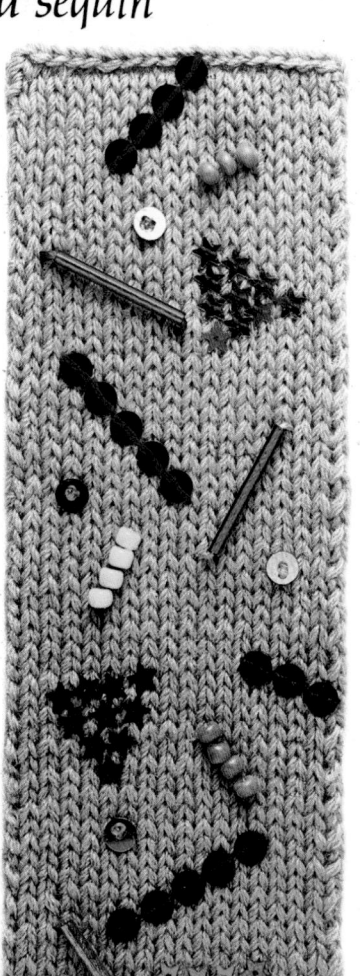

Thread bead onto yarn and insert needle through same hole. Make a stitch slightly longer than bead length. Pull firmly and repeat.

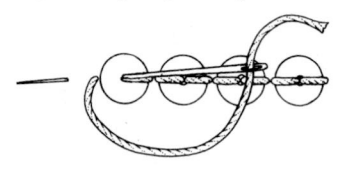

Bring needle through middle of sequin. Work back stitch over RS bringing needle out to far L, ready to thread on next sequin.

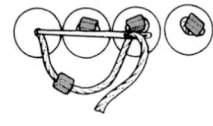

Thread sequin and bead onto yarn. Insert needle through middle of sequin and draw through a short distance away. Pull firmly.

Glistening beads and sequins contrast well with the softness of knitting yarn and may be sewn onto fine knitteds with matching sewing thread or fine embroidery yarns. Sew beads and sequins with a firm stitch but keep stranding threads on wrong side short and relaxed and an even tension throughout.

Free=style

Materials Stranded or soft embroidery cotton for a pretty look.
Uses Single motif for twinset front panel, or all-over repeat for baby's dress yoke or crib cover.

1 *Make short st. Loop yarn under needle, draw through, repeat.*

2 *Twist needle twice around thread, insert near starting point.*

3 *From L to R, work small even sts on line.*

1 **Buttonhole stitch**
2 **French knot**
3 **Stem stitch**

4 **Single chain stitch**

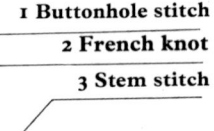

4 *Bring needle out at top. Insert into same hole; work short st with loop under needle. Make tying st, repeat.*

Use a fine blunt-ended tapestry needle and work with a relaxed tension throughout. Avoid making long stranding threads on wrong side which would restrict the elasticity of your knitting. Generally it is better to start and finish working one color at a time, fastening off by neatly running thread through wrong side of embroidery.

Index

Acknowledgments

Contributors
Marnie Newey
Janet Swift
Mary Tebbs

Assistants
Maggie Elliott
Gilly Squires

Artist
John Hutchinson

Photographers
Ian O'Leary
Steve Oliver

Typesetting
Contact Graphics Ltd

Reproduction
F. E. Burman Ltd